LECTIN FREE DIET

A Step by Step Guide to Prepare Healthy Recipes to Fight Inflammation

(The Complete Guide of Lectin Free Instant Cooking Book)

Matthew Sorrell

Published by Alex Howard

© **Matthew Sorrell**

All Rights Reserved

Lectin Free Diet: A Step by Step Guide to Prepare Healthy Recipes to Fight Inflammation (The Complete Guide of Lectin Free Instant Cooking Book)

ISBN 978-1-990169-16-8

All rights reserved. No part of this guide may be reproduced in any form without permission in writing from the publisher except in the case of brief quotations embodied in critical articles or reviews.

Legal & Disclaimer

The information contained in this book is not designed to replace or take the place of any form of medicine or professional medical advice. The information in this book has been provided for educational and entertainment purposes only.

The information contained in this book has been compiled from sources deemed reliable, and it is accurate to the best of the Author's knowledge; however, the Author cannot guarantee its accuracy and validity and cannot be held liable for any errors or omissions. Changes are periodically made to this book. You must consult your doctor or get professional medical advice before using any of the suggested remedies, techniques, or information in this book.

Table of contents

PART 1 1

INTRODUCTION 2

CHAPTER 1: WHAT IS LECTIN AND WHY IS IT UNHEALTHY FOR YOUR BODY. 4

WHERE DO LECTINS COME FROM? 4
WHAT MAKES LECTIN UNHEALTHY IN HUMANS 5
WHAT IS AN INSTANT POT AND WHY IS IT IMPORTANT? 5

CHAPTER 2: LECTIN-FREE RECIPES 10

RECIPE #1: INSTANT POT HOMEMADE PUMPKIN PUREE 10
RECIPE #2: KNOEPHLA SOUP 11
RECIPE #3: INSTANT POT TACO MEAT 12
RECIPE #4: DEEP-FRIED BUTTERFIELD SHRIMP 14
RECIPE #5: GOAT CURRY IN A HURRY 15
RECIPE #6: INSTANT POT DEEP-FRY PRETZEL COATED FRIED FISH 16
RECIPE #7: THE LOW CARB, INSTANT POT JAMAICAN JERK PORK ROAST 17
RECIPE #8: THE INSTANT POT DOUBLE BEAN AND HAM SOUP 18
RECIPE #9: INSTANT POT MAC AND CHEESE WITH HAM AND PEAS 19
RECIPE #10: FRIED VENISON BACK-STRAP 20
RECIPE #11: THE DELICIOUS FRIED FISH TACOS 20
RECIPE #12: THE CHINESE BROCCOLI RECIPE 22
RECIPE #13: GAMBAS PIL-PIL (THE CHILEAN PRAWNS) 23
RECIPE #14: THE INSTANT POT PINEAPPLE-COCONUT-LIME RICE 24
RECIPE #15: KETOGENIC INSTANT POT SOUP 25
RECIPE #16: THE INSTANT POT THAI RED CURRY WITH CHICKEN 26
RECIPE #17: THE HONEY SPICED CAJUN CHICKEN 28
RECIPE #18: THE INSTANT POT MUSHROOM RISOTTO 29
RECIPE #19: THE KNACK TOFFEE 31
RECIPE #20: SAVOY CABBAGE WITH CREAM SAUCE 32
RECIPE #21: FRIED TERIYAKI CHICKEN WINGS 33
RECIPE #22: PORK ROAST WITH MUSHROOM GRAVY 34
RECIPE #23: THE FISH BATTER WITH "NEWCASTLE" BROWN ALE 35
RECIPE #24: THE INSTANT POT PALEO EGG ROLL SOUP 36

- Recipe #25: The Instant Pot Fall Harvest Pork Soup (French Onion Soup) 37
- Recipe #26: The Sicilian Stuffed Artichoke 38
- Recipe #27: The Steamed Artichoke 39
- Recipe #28: Instant Pot Shredded Chicken 40
- Recipe #29: The Family-Friendly Amish Chicken And Corn Soup 41
- Recipe #30: The Ground Beef Chili 42
- Recipe #31: The Japanese Style Deep-Fried Shrimp 44
- Recipe #32: Instant Pot Cooker Italian Beef 45
- Recipe #33: The Instant Pot Coconut Orange Rice Pudding 46
- Recipe #34: The Chicken And Veggie Miso Soup 46
- Recipe #35: Artichokes With Sautéed Navy Beans 49
- Recipe #36: The Instant Pot Baked Beef Soup 50
- Recipe #37: The Country Chicken Stew 51
- Recipe #38: The Tasty Instant Pot Aromatic Lamp Chops 52
- Recipe #39: The Instant Pot Vegetarian Curry Soup 53
- Recipe #40: Instant Pot Stir Fries With Beef And Green Beans 55
- Recipe #41: The Traditional Instant Pot Pho Ga Soup 56
- Recipe #42: Crab Meat With Asparagus Soup 58
- Recipe #43: Scintillating Fried Squid With Pineapple 59
- Recipe #44: Instant Pot Vietnamese Eggplant With Spicy Sauce 60
- Recipe #45: The Instant Pot Chickpea Curry 61
- Recipe #46: Artichoke Salsa 62
- Recipe #47: The Instant Pot Alfredo Sauce With Artichoke 63
- Recipe #48: The 15-Minute Barbecue Chicken Soup 64
- Recipe #49: The Instant Pot Salsa Chicken 65
- Recipe #50: Instant Pot Rosemary Lemon Chicken 66
- Recipe #51: Arctic Char With A Bed Of Kale 67
- Recipe #52: The Red Snapper Caribbean Recipe 68
- Recipe #53: Instant Pot Mini-Lemon Cheesecakes 69
- Recipe #54: Artichoke In Garlic And Olive Oil Sauce 71
- Recipe #55: Porridge Served With Cinnamon 72
- Recipe #56: Instant Pot Prosciutto Fritters (Polpette Di Patate Fritte) 73
- Recipe #57: Sautéed Navy Beans Artichoke 74
- Recipe #58: Delicious Egg Scrambles With Spinach 75
- Recipe #59: Garlic Sautéed Artichoke 76
- Recipe #60: The Mediterranean Fried Cabbage Served With Bacon And Onion ... 77

Recipe #61: The Steamed-Cooked Artichoke 78
Recipe #62: Creamy Toasted Garlic Mushrooms 79
Recipe #63: The Lentils And Spinach Mix 80
Recipe #64: Artichoke Tetrazzini 81
Recipe #65: The Vegetarian Cassoulet 82
Recipe #66: Coconut Little Kiss (Beijinho De Coco) 83
Recipe #67: Chicken With Artichoke 84
Recipe #68: The Instant Pot Cheese Cake 86
Recipe #69: The Lifesaver BBQ Pressure Chicken Wings 88
Recipe 70: The Instant Pot Deviled Eggs 89
Recipe #71: Instant Pot Korean Ribs 90
Recipe #72: The Classic Instant Pot Soy Sauce Eggs 92
Recipe #73: The Instant Pot Chinese Braised Beef Shank 93
Recipe #74: The Cheese Beer-Burger Dip 94
Recipe #75: The Mason Jar Steel Cut Oats In Pressure Cooker 95
Recipe #76: The Steel Cut Oats 96
Recipe #77: Instant Pot Lentil Sloppy Joes 97
Recipe #78: Instant Pot Avocado And Tunas Tapas 98
Recipe #79: Instant Pot Espicanas Con Garbanzos (Spinach With Garbanzos Beans) 99
Recipe #80: The Instant Pot Sautéed Marinated Shrimp 100

TWO-WEEK MEAL PLAN FOR LECTIN-FREE BODY 102

Week 1 Lectin-Free Meal Plan 102
Week 2 Lectin-Free Meal Plan 104

CONCLUSION 106

PART 2 107

INTRODUCTION 108

CHAPTER 1: ESSENTIALS OF THE LECTIN FREE DIET 109

CHAPTER 2: EASING INTO THE LECTIN FREE DIET 119

CHAPTER 3: EASY-TO-FOLLOW BREAKFAST RECIPES 122

Mesmerizing Cauliflower Pudding 122
Cool Prosciutto Cane 123

Simple And Straightforward Broccoli 124
Easy Going Mushroom Bowl 125
Appetizing Chicken Balls 126
Very Nutty Faux "Oatmeal" 127
Early Morning Good Sausage Meatloaf 128
Creamy Nice Broccoli Casserole 129
Bacon And Kale 130

CHAPTER 4: MOUTH-WATERING FISH AND SEAFOOD RECIPES 131

Shrimp And Sausage Bowl 131
Tasty Sweet Chili Tilapia Dish 133
Salmon And Broccoli Medley 134
Sharp Garlic And Butter Swordfish 135
Authentic Ginger Tilapia 136
Coconut Shrimp 138
Asparagus Tilapia Dish 139
Amazing Salmon Curry 140
Crazy Slow Salmon Fillet 142

CHAPTER 5: GRACEFUL LECTIN FREE MEAT RECIPES 143

Pork And Cabbage Platter 143
Big Time Buffalo Wings And Cauliflower * 144
Harissa Beef 144
Thick Artichoke Pork Chops 146
The Swedish Pork Roast 148
Succulent Pot Roast 150
Cilantro And Lime (Shredded) Pork 151
Easy Beef Brisket 152
Dijon Pork Chops 154

CHAPTER 6: HEALTHY VEGAN AND VEGETARIAN RECIPES 155

Hearty Asparagus Salad 155
Multi-Colored Brussels 157
Zucchini And Artichoke Platter 158
Heart "Beets" In A Pot 159
A Platter Of Leafy Greens 160
Simple Zucchini Pasta Pesto 161

Super Baked Apple Dish 162
Delicious Root Vegetable Dish 163
Feisty Potato Grain 164
Caramelized Onion With Dope Garlic 165
Delicious Ginger Sweet Potatoes 166

CHAPTER 7: FLAVORED SOUP AND STEWS RECIPES 167

Smoked Paprika Soup 167
Lovely Cabbage And Leek Delight 169
Tongue Teasing Mushroom Soup 171
Light Carrot Soup 172
Inspiring Broccoli And Leek Soup 173
Elegant Cauliflower Soup 174
Awesome Beef Stew 176
Blissful Turkey Spinach Soup 177
Bacon And Spinach Soup 178
Amazing Sausage Soup 179
Authentic Chard Soup 180
Ultimate Cauliflower Soup 181

CHAPTER 8: GREAT SNACK AND DESSERTS RECIPES 182

Whole Roasted Garlic 182
Juicy Caramelized Onion 183
Hearty Steamed Sweet Potatoes 184
Maple Dressed Carrots 185
Lovely Potato Hash 186
Herbed Mushrooms 187

CONCLUSION 188

Part 1

Introduction

Generally, aflatoxins are not good for the body and they must be eliminated as soon as possible before they create complications especially in the digestive tract of the human system. High levels of toxic substances such as Lectin has been linked to indigestion or slow digestion and the irritation of the digestive tract- all these issues can lead to lower absorption of nutrients into the body as digestion becomes hindered significantly.

Humans are highly susceptible to a number of long term problems caused by lectin. Unfortunately, lectin is found in so many food products which include some vegetable oils we used in cooking. When your digestive system is not in working order, you will suffer from nutritional deficiencies, your body for instance will absorb less nutrients that wouldn't have benefitted it in so many ways.

In addition to absorbing less essential vitamins, minerals, and Phyto-nutrients, your, the ability of your body to eliminate more waste will be affected through the damage caused by lectin and when lectin continues to buildup without being eliminated, it can cause long term damages to vital organs. In addition to this, the buildup of lectin and other toxins in your body can also make weight loss more difficult, and when it becomes difficult to lose weight, you will feel sluggish day-in-day-out, and that will even make exercising more difficult.

Fortunately, one of the smartest ways of eliminating lectin from your diet is through the cooking method. Though, it is ideal to reduce lectin by eliminating foods rich in the substance, but sometimes, it can be very difficult eliminating all food items contain lectin. Instant pot for instance helps in destroying most of the bio-chemical components of lectin through the application of high pressure cooking method that ensure a complete heat circulation in and around the food being prepared, thus making the food more wholesome and more nutritious, while preserving the essential nutrients.

Chapter 1: What Is Lectin And Why Is It Unhealthy For Your Body

Lectins are carbohydrate-binding protein, found in mostly grains and legumes. Lectins are found to damage the linings of the human digestive system and that is one of the primary reasons they must be avoided.

Lectins are actually found in almost all the foods you can mention, and most especially in Legumes and grains. The frequent consumption of lectin can scar the lining of the digestive system, especially when it is consumed too frequently. When the control of lectin is not controlled, it can lead to gut permeability which can lead to the leaching of food particles through the walls of the intestines and may also trigger auto-immune disorder.

Where Do Lectins Come From?

Virtually all plants and animals contain Lectin, hence they are found in abundance in lots of foods. They are special proteins that play active roles in the physiological functions in the plants and the human body. In plants for instance, Lectin helps the cells and molecule stick together to boost the plant's immunity against certain infestations and pests.

Though, nearly all foods contain lectin, but only 30% of foods contain significant amounts that can have some negative effects in the body. Most lectins can be found in legumes such as beans, soy beans and peanuts. They can also be found in grains, dairy, and sea foods.

Lectins are believed to take active part in strengthening the defense mechanisms in plants, they specifically create unpalatable tastes and odor that dissuades animals from eating them. It is very important to be careful when consuming raw plant foods and their processed forms, Ricin is a poisonous form of lectin that is found in castor oil plant, this substance can lead to death after long term usage.

What Makes Lectin Unhealthy In Humans

The main reason why lectins trigger problems in humans is because we have problems digesting the substances. Lectins are highly resistance to enzymes in the human body, which means they can easily pass through the stomach without change or digestion. Lectins are very sticky in nature and that is the reason they attach easily to the intestinal walls. Once they are attached to the intestinal walls in humans, they disrupt daily routine maintenance of the body by the cells and tissues in the body, causing daily wear and tear that will gradually worsen in the intestines. Lectins also cause a gradually reduction in the absorption of nutrients that the body needs.

In order to avoid accumulating lectins rapidly in the body, you must avoid the consumption of uncooked raw legumes, most especially the kidney beans. As a matter of fact, the consumption of raw kidney beans can cause lectin poison, which in turn can cause death on the long run.

When you consume lectin on the long run, it can result in gut permeability and when the gut is damaged, some unwanted materials may easily move through them. The increase in gut permeability is referred to as "leaky guts". When lectins has successfully leaked into the blood stream, it will interact with glycol-proteins found in the cells, lectin will also interact with antibodies that form the immune system – this situation can trigger immune reactions to the presence of lectin and in this case, the immune system may begin to attack its own component structures, thus creating regular auto-immune disorders.

What Is An Instant Pot And Why Is It Important?

Instant pot can best be described as a multi-cooker that can perform so many things at the same time with the switch of a button, hence it can make cooking a whole lot faster. This Instant pot can perform the duties of a slow cooker, alongside the duties of an electric pressure cooker, plus steamer, Sautee and browning pan.

With a single appliance that can perform more than 7 different jobs, you will be impressed about the speed at which you can prepare a weight loss ketogenic meal within few minutes. This appliance is thus perfect for busy mothers, hungry adults who have little or no time to prepare meals that will take very long period of time.

Beginner users of the Instant pot will think the device is too good to be true and may probably end up malfunctioning sooner or later, but that is a lie- the Instant pot is designed to last for decades even with continuous usage.

The Instant pot cooker is designed to make cooking faster, and more convenient. To make use of the device, simply add water and your food component inside the pressure cooking pot which is the inner pot, then lock the lid top in place and make sure the valve is set at the sealing/pressure cooking position. Set the pressure cooking button at the short cooking time and watch as the pressure cooker completes the job.

The instant pot has 16 different settings, hence the front of the device looks like Dashboard because it is where you can switch from one setting to another. Each button you find in the front, represents specific type of cooking, and they work because they have specific pre-set cooking times that will make your cooking a lot easier.

The settings on each button also indicates whether the pot will remained locked to capture the steam while you pressure-cook, or if it will be using the regular pot cooking without the need to use different pressure.

For most soups, bean and chilli, the average cooking time in the instant pot is 30 minutes (at high pressure setting. For meat and stew, and multigrain cooking, the average cooking time at high pressure setting is 35 minutes. For poultry, cooking time is 15 minutes, at high pressure, and for porridge, the average cooking time is 20 minutes at high temperature.

There are different Instant pot models measured by their capacities and sizes, these vary from between 5 quart capacity 900W to the 8 quart capacity 1200W.

There are so many reasons why you need to consider using the Instant pot whole 30. These include the following;

#1: Instant pot saves time and energy

With instant pot, foods are cooked speedily, with the use of pressure cooking methods. The instant cooker can reduce cooking time by as much as 70% when compared to other methods. Less water is used in this 100% insulated external water pot, and instant pot remain the best energy saving cooking appliance in the world today.

#2: Preserves nutrients and produce better tasting foods

Heat is distributed more evenly with instant pot cooking, hence the use of an instant pressure cooker in preparing the whole 30 recipes will ensure that nutrients are quickly and deeply distributed.

With instant pot, you don't have to immerse the food in water, the steam available is enough to distribute heat evenly and quickly and for this reason essential and vital nutrient such as minerals and vitamins are not leached into water.

Since the food are surrounded by steam from the instant pot, there will be no oxidation, hence the food can keep its original flavor. Electric pressure cooker makes use of a fully sealed cooking techniques, hence your delicate veggies such as broccoli, and asparagus, will retain their bright colors.

#3: Instant pot destroys harmful micro-organisms in food

With the aid of the instant pot pressure cooker, food is prepared at a temperature higher than the boiling point of water, and for this reason, all harmful micro-organisms are destroyed within the shortest period of time, and these include the pathogenic bacteria and parasites.

Instant pot pressure cookers have been used for decades as sterilizers, especially for jam pots as well as glass baby bottles. Instant pot Pressure cookers are also used in treating water.

Some food items can carry huge loads of aflatoxins, which are naturally occurring mycotoxins produced by numerous species of the fungi – Aspergillus. Many foods can develop mycotoxins due to improper storage conditions such as temperatures and humidity. Aflatoxins in food can trigger a number of diseases and infections, including liver cancer, especially when the food is not prepared very well. Aside from liver cancer, aflatoxins can trigger other problems such as diarrhea, constipation and general and slow functioning of the vital organs.

Heating foods to the boiling point will not destroy all aflatoxins because many of them possess strong resistance to heat. Researches conducted by some Korean researches have confirmed that the use of instant pot in heating food can reduce the concentration of aflatoxins to the safest levels.

When cooking the Mexican chili for instance, the kidney beans used in this recipe contains a huge concentration of aflatoxin, however, boiling these kidney beans at high temperatures in instant pot for about 10 minutes can actually cause the destruction of the aflatoxins.

Instant pot cooking will degrade most lectins present in food

It is practically impossible to avoid lectin because it is found in almost all food components. Many professional nutritionists recommend that legumes and grains should be avoided in diets, but this can be practically impossible, considering the fact that whole grains form part of most staple foods.

An ideal alternative is to boil legumes for instance, as boiling can eliminate more than 90% of lectin. The use of instant pot cooker can eliminate 99.9% of lectin in legumes, grains and other categories of food. Aside from cooking, preparing food through fermentation, soaking, and sprouting can also eliminate lectin. Fermentation for instance can help digest lectin through the activities of Probiotics(helpful bacteria), while sprouting and soaking will help to dissolve lectin and render them inactive.

Chapter 2: Lectin-Free Recipes

Since most foods contain Lectin, it makes a lot of sense to choose the healthiest ingredients, keeping in mind that Instant pot cooking will destroy most lectins and render the remaining lectin content too weak to cause any problem in the body.

Recipe #1: Instant Pot Homemade Pumpkin Puree

(Total time: 30 minutes, serving: 2-3)

Ingredient

- 4 lbs. of pie pumpkin,
- 1 cup of water.

Direction

1. Remove stem from pumpkin. Place the rack of steamer basket at the bottom of the instant pot and add the water. Place your pumpkin on the rack or basket, and make sure the lid of the instant pot can be closed without it touching the top of the pumpkin.
2. Seal your instant pot and cook the pumpkin for 13 minutes, then let the pressure releases itself naturally. Gently lift the pumpkin out of the pressure cooker before placing it on a cutting board or plate and let it cool for about 2 minutes.
3. Slice the pumpkin in halves and then remove the seeds before you goop and peel the skin.
4. Blend the pumpkin inside a blender or food processor, and add a tablespoon of water. Make sure it is smooth after blending.
5. Store it in the refrigerator until needed.

Recipe #2: Knoephla Soup

(Total time: 30 minutes, servings: 4)
Ingredients:
- 1 cup of celery (diced),
- 1 ½ cups of carrots (diced),
- ½ a bag of spätzle dumping,
- 2 cans of chicken soup ,
- 2 cups of chicken broth,
- ½ tablespoons each of pepper and salt.

Directions
1. Add all your ingredients except chicken soup into the instant pot, and cover with the lid before you close the pressure valve. Then set the time at 15 minutes at high pressure to cook the soup.
2. Slowly release the valves before you open the instant pot lid.
3. Serve immediately.

Recipe #3: Instant Pot Taco Meat

(Total time: 25 minutes, servings: 2)
Ingredients:
- 2lbs. of ground beef,
- 4 tablespoons of olive oil,
- 2 red diced onions,
- 3 green diced bell peppers,
- 5 minced garlic cloves,
- 2 teaspoons of chili powder,
- 2 teaspoons of oregano,
- 1 teaspoon of salt,
- 1 teaspoon of basil (dried),
- ½ a teaspoon of turmeric,
- ½ a teaspoon of black pepper,
- 1 teaspoon of paprika,
- 1 teaspoon of cumin,
- ½ a teaspoon of cayenne,
- ½ a teaspoon of chipotle powder,
- Cilantro (for garnishing).

Directions
1. Add all ingredients (except the ground beef), into the instant pot, then press the "sauté" button and stir-fry for about 6 minutes.
2. Add the brown beef unto the pot and cook further for 2 minutes until it turns brown.
3. Secure the lid and then close the pressure valve and cook further for 10 minutes at high pressure.

4. Let the pressure release from the instant pot naturally, once the met is done cooking or simply perform the quick release option.

5. Open the lid and garnish with the cilantro when serving.

Recipe #4: Deep-Fried Butterfield Shrimp

(Total time: 35 minutes, servings: 4)

Ingredients:
- 1 lb. of large shrimp (peeled, deveined and butter-flied),
- 2 large eggs,
- 5 cup of oil (for deep frying),
- 2 cup of bread crumbs(fresh),
- 1 quart of water, and
- 1 ½ cup of corn starch.

Directions

1. Press the "sauté" button on the instant pot before adding the ingredients (except bread crumbs). Sauté for 10 minutes then press the "cancel" button

2. Add the bread crumbs before pressing the "deep fry" option on the instant pot and fry for about 15 minutes.

3. Serve immediately.

Recipe #5: Goat Curry In A Hurry

(Total time: 25 minutes, servings: 2)

Ingredients:

- 2 tablespoons of oil (avocado oil preferred),
- 2 lbs. of goat or lamb (bone-in-goat preferred),
- 2 diced onions,
- 1 ½ inch knob of minced fresh ginger, and
- 3 cloves of minced garlic, and
- 4 whole cloves or, a teaspoon of any spice of your choice

Directions

1. Press on the "sauté" button in the instant pot, then add the oil alongside the goat meat unto the pot. Add the onion, ginger, garlic and the spice once the meat begins to brown.

2. Pour in the remaining spice (if there is any left), then secure the lid and close the pressure valve. Cook for about 15 minutes.

3. Let the pressure releases itself naturally after cooking, and serve immediately.

Recipe #6: Instant Pot Deep-Fry Pretzel Coated Fried Fish

(Total time: 30 minutes, serving: 4)

Ingredients:

- 1 quart of oil,
- ¾ of a cup of all-purpose flour,
- 1 teaspoon of salt,
- ½ a teaspoon of ground black pepper,
- ¾ of a cup of crushed pretzels,
- 2 large eggs,
- 1 lb. of frozen cod fillets (thawed).

Directions

1. Spread the fish on a plate and then rob the flour on them.

2. Press the "Sauté" button on the instant pot and then add all ingredients along with the fish. Sauté for about 25 minutes under high pressure, and while the valve is tightly closed.

3. Release the valve and cool the deep-fried fish for about 2 minute before serving.

Recipe #7: The Low Carb, Instant Pot Jamaican Jerk Pork Roast

(Total time: 50 minutes, servings: 12)

Ingredients:
- 4 lbs., of pork shoulder,
- ¼ of a cup of jerk spice blend (no sugar),
- 1 tablespoon of olive oil, and
- ½ a cup of beef stock or broth.

Directions

1. Rub the pork with olive oil before coating with the spice blend.
2. Set the instant pot to the "sauté" option, and brown the meet in all sides.
3. Add the broth, then seal the top of the Instant pot and cook at high pressure for 35 minutes.
4. Release the pressure of the instant pot after cooking, then shred and serve immediately.

Recipe #8: The Instant Pot Double Bean And Ham Soup

(Total time: 1 hour 10 minutes, servings: 6)

Ingredients:
- 2 cups of navy beans (dry),
- 1 large onion (chopped)
- 2 cups of chicken broth,
- 2 stalks celery (chopped)
- 2 cups of water,
- 1 can (16 ounce) of pork and beans (undrained),
- 1 cup of chopped ham,
- 2 large carrots(chopped), and
- ½ teaspoon each of salt and pepper

Directions

1. Add the navy beans alongside the chicken broth, carrots, onion, water and celery into the instant pot, then seal the pressure cooker and turn the knob to "sauté" and set the timer at 45 minutes.
2. Release the pressure manually when the timer is completed.
3. Remove the lid and stir the pork, beans and the ham, before you season with salt and pepper.

Recipe #9: Instant Pot Mac And Cheese With Ham And Peas

(Total time: 44 minutes, serving: 6)
Ingredients:
- 4 cups of water,
- 1 pack (16 ounces) of elbow macaroni,
- 1 tablespoon of dry mustard powder,
- 1 teaspoon of salt,
- 1 tablespoon of hot sauce (optional),
- 1 can of evaporated milk (12 ounce),
- 1/3 of a cup of whole milk,
- 2 tablespoons of unsalted butter,
- 2 cups of shredded 2%milk cheddar cheese,
- 1 cup of shredded Monterrey Jack cheese,
- 1 cup of diced cooked ham,
- ½ cup of frozen peas (defrosted), and
- ½ a teaspoon each of salt and pepper (ground).

Directions
1. Add the water, with the macaroni, mustard powder, salt and hot sauce inside the instant pot. Close the pot and put the lid. Set the timer at 4 minutes, and set it at high pressure.
2. As the cooking is done, release the pressure slowly, with the aid of the quick release option. Unlock before removing the lid. Switch the function to low Sauté option by pressing the "sauté" once. Make sure you stir the macaroni to remove clumps.
3. Stir in the evaporated milk alongside the butter and milk into the pot. Add the cheddar and Monterrey cheese gradually and stir continuously until they become melted. Add the ham and peas before seasoning with salt and pepper.

Recipe #10: Fried Venison Back-Strap

(Total time: 45 minutes, servings: 8)

Ingredients:
- 1 (lbs.) venison blackstrap, cut into ¼ inch thick slices,
- 2 cups of milk,
- 2 tablespoons of hot pepper sauce,
- 2 large eggs,
- ½ a cup of milk,
- 3 cup of all-purpose flour,
- 2 tablespoons of salt,
- 1 tablespoon of black pepper (ground),
- 3 cups of vegetable oil.

Directions

1. Get a shallow bowl and inside place the venison back-strap, then pour in the hot sauce and milk, stir for the venison to coat, and marinate for about an hour. Get a shallow bowl and inside whisk the eggs and milk. Get a separate bowl and inside stir together the flour, pepper and salt.

2. Mix everything together and add into the sauce pan, then secure the lid and valve before choosing the "Sauté" option and choose 25 minutes cooking time.

3. Once the cooking is completed, let the instant pot pressure releases itself automatically. Cool for few minutes before serving.

Recipe #11: The Delicious Fried Fish Tacos

(Total time: 45 minutes, servings: 10)

Ingredients:

- 1 cup of all-purpose flour,
- ½ a teaspoon of salt,
- 1 ½ lbs. of cubed cod fillets,
- 1 quart of vegetable oil,
- 20 corn tortillas (6 inch),
- 5 cups of shredded cabbage,
- 1 cup of mayonnaise,
- ¼ of a cup of salsa,
- 1 lime (cut into wedges).

Directions

1. Get a shallow bowl, and inside, whisk together the flour, and salt. Rinse the fish and pat it dry, then cut them into 10 equal pieces.

2. Add the mix into the instant pot pressure cooker alongside other ingredients. Close the lid, and set at sauté option before setting the cooking temperature at 25 minutes.

3. Once the cooking is done, simply allow the pressure to release naturally – this will take some 10 to 15 minutes, then gently un-lid the pot and pour the recipe into a serving bowl.

Recipe #12: The Chinese Broccoli Recipe

(Total time: 25 minutes, servings: 4)

Ingredients:

- 1 lbs. of Broccoli,
- ¼ of a cup of butter or margarine,
- ¼ cup of water,
- 1 tablespoon of soy sauce,
- 1 tablespoon of soy sauce,
- 1 cup of celery (thinly sliced),
- 1 can of 5-ounce water chestnuts (sliced and drained),
- 1 ½ tablespoons of sesame seeds.

Directions

1. Trim out the outer leaves and ends of the broccoli, then cut the stalks and florets into 2-inch lengths before slicing lengthwise into halves.

2. Add the trimmed broccoli alongside other ingredients to the pan of the instant pot and close the lid before setting the high pressure and cooking time at 20 minutes. Make sure you choose "sauté" option on the instant pot.

3. Once the cooking time is completed, allow the pressure cooker to release itself (it should take about 10 minutes). Pour the broccoli recipe in a serving bowl.

Recipe #13: Gambas Pil-Pil (The Chilean Prawns)

(Total time: 32 minutes, servings: 6)

Ingredients:
- 10 cloves of garlic (slightly crushed and peeled),
- 3 tablespoons of brandy or pisco,
- ½ a teaspoon of salt,
- ½ a cup of grapeseed oil or olive oil,
- 1 ½ lbs. of large shrimp (de-veined and peeled),
- ½ teaspoon of cayenne pepper
- 1 Cacho de Cabra pepper (or Anaheim pepper), it must be seeded and cut into ½ inch pieces, and
- 1 lime (cut into wedges)

Directions

1. Get a bowl, and inside, place the garlic cloves and the grapeseed oil, and pour into the instant pot. Set the cooking time at 5 minutes at high pressure after covering the pot with lid and securing the valve. Cook until the garlic cloves turn golden brown, and the oil has become hot.
2. Add the remaining ingredients and set at "sauté" option and set cooking temperature at 15 minutes.
3. Make use of the quick release option after the cooking and pour into a serving bowl.

Recipe #14: The Instant Pot Pineapple-Coconut-Lime Rice

(Total time: 33 minutes, serving: 4)
Ingredients:
- 1 ½ cups of uncooked long-grain white rice,
- 1 cup of water,
- 1 (8 ounce) of undrained crushed pineapple,
- ¾ of a cup of coconut milk,
- ¼ of a teaspoon of red pepper flakes,
- 1 lime (juiced and zested).

Directions

1. Rinse the water clearly and place the drained rice into the instant pot. Add the water and pineapple chunks alongside the juice, coconut milk, and red pepper flakes. Place the pot lid and lock it in place.

2. Turn on the instant pot and choose the manual setting and high pressure. Set the timer at 3 minutes and after cooking time, simply let the pressure release itself naturally (this will take about 20 minutes).

3. Stir in the lime zest and juice and serve.

Recipe #15: Ketogenic Instant Pot Soup

(Total time: 58 minutes, serving: 6)
Ingredients:
- 1 tablespoon of olive oil,
- 1 yellow onion (diced),
- 2 cloves of minced garlic,
- 1 head of cauliflower (coarsely chopped),
- 1 green chopped bell pepper,
- 1 tablespoon of onion powder,
- ½ teaspoon each for salt and black pepper,
- 1 container (32 ounce) of chicken stock,
- 2 cups of shredded cheddar cheese,
- 1 cup of half-and –half,
- 1 tablespoon of Dijon Mustard,
- 4 dashes of hot pepper sauce.

Directions

1. Turn on the instant pot, and choose the "sauté" function. Add the olive oil and then the onion and garlic and sauté until brown- this should take about 3 minutes. Add the green bell pepper, alongside cauliflower onion powder, pepper and salt, then pour in the chicken stock and close the lid before selecting the "soup" function. Set the timer at 15 minutes.

2. Make use of the quick release option to release the pressure after cooking (this should take about 5 minutes). Unlock and take off the lid before adding the cheddar cheese, half-and-half, turkey bacon, hot sauce, and Dijon mustard. Select the "sauté" function again, and cook for about 5 minutes until it becomes bubbly.

Recipe #16: The Instant Pot Thai Red Curry With Chicken

(Total time: 1 hour 12 minute, serving: 6)
Ingredients:
- 1 tablespoon of olive oil,
- ½ diced onion,
- 2 cloves of minced garlic,
- 1 stalk sliced celery,
- ½ a cup of chopped carrots,
- 2 boneless chicken breasts (sliced),
- 1 can (14 ounce) of coconut milk,
- 2 tablespoons of fish sauce,
- ½ a cup of water,
- ½ a cup of frozen peas,
- 3 tablespoons of red curry paste,
- 2 tablespoons of brown sugar,
- 3 chicken bouillon cubes (crushed).

Directions
1. Add the olive oil to the instant pot and put 'sauté' mode before heating the oil. Add the onion and garlic, then sauté further until they become soft (3 minutes). Add your celery and cook further until they turn bright green. Add the carrots and stir.
2. Place the chicken slices on top of the sautéed veggies, then pour the coconut milk on top of the chicken then add the fish sauce before you allow the liquid to boil (5 minutes). Mix in the water, peas, brown sugar, curry paste, and bouillon cubes.

3. Place the lid on the instant pot, and bring it to high pressure. Cook further for 12 minutes and release the pressure manually once the cooking time is reached. And then Service immediately

Recipe #17: The Honey Spiced Cajun Chicken

(Total time: 25 minutes, serving: 8)
Ingredients:

- 10 oz. of pounded chicken breast,
- Cooked linguini,
- 3 sliced large mushrooms,
- 2 tablespoons of mustard,
- ½ teaspoon of red pepper
- 4 tablespoons of honey, and
- 3 .oz. of cream

Directions

1. Pat the chicken inside the seasonings.

2. Power on the instant pot and add the chicken, alongside all other ingredients into the pan. Close the lid and secure the valves and set the timer at 20 minutes. Make sure you select "sauté" option.

3. Once the time has lapsed, simply allow the instant pot to ease the pressure manually, and transfer the chicken into a serving bowl or plate.

Recipe #18: The Instant Pot Mushroom Risotto

(Total time: 50 minutes, serving: 4)
Ingredients:
- ¼ of a cup of unsalted butter,
- ¼ of a cup of olive oil,
- 3 cup of diced mushrooms,
- 1 cup of chopped onion,
- 1 sprig of rosemary,
- 1 ½ cups of Arborio rice,
- 1 quart of a chicken stock,
- ½ of a cup of grated Parmesan cheese, and
- ½ teaspoon each of salt and pepper.

Directions

1. Press the "sauté" function on the instant pot, and then add the butter along with the olive oil. Stir for about 2 minutes until the butter melts, then add the mushroom and cook further while stirring occasionally (3 minutes). Stir in your onion and cook for extra 2 minutes, then add the rosemary sprig before cooking for 1 minute further.

2. Stir the rice into the pot and let them be coated with the butter and olive mix. Simmer for about 3 minutes before you pour the chicken stock, then stir to scrape the sides of the pot before you simmer again for 1 minute.

3. Close the lid and lock it, then turn on the venting knob at "sealed". Choose the manual function and set timer at 6 minutes. Choose high pressure.

4. Tap on the venting knob occasionally with a spatula or wooden spoon, then stand back and turn the knob to point at the vent. Remove the lid once the pressure has been released (5 minutes).

5. Stir the Risotto for about 1 minute, until it becomes creamy, then remove the rosemary sprig. Season with the salt and pepper before stirring in the parmesan cheese.

Recipe #19: The Knack Toffee

(Total time: 45 minutes, Servings: 48)

Ingredients:
- ¾ of a cup of light molasses,
- ¾ of a cup of heavy whipping cream,
- 2 teaspoons of cocoa powder (unsweetened),
- ¼ of a cup of chopped almonds,
- 1 teaspoon of vanilla extract, and
- ¾ of a cup of white sugar.

Direction

1. Mix all the ingredients (except vanilla extract and almond), inside the instant pot and bring the mix to a boil (20 minutes). Stir in the vanilla and almond.

2. Spoon the candy into some small paper candy cups, then cool it to room temperature before you store in air-tight container at room temperature.

Recipe #20: Savoy Cabbage With Cream Sauce

(Total time: 19 minutes, serving 4-6)
Ingredients:

- 1 cup of diced bacon or lardons,
- 1 large chopped onion,
- 2 cup of bone broth,
- 1 medium size head choy cabbage (finely chopped),
- ¼ of a teaspoon of mace (or nutmeg),
- ½ a can of coconut milk (200 mls),
- 1 bay leaf,
- ½ teaspoon of salt ,
- 2 tablespoons of parsley flakes.

Directions

1. Press the "sauté" option on the instant pot, and let the inner pot heat up. Add the bacon and onion, until they become crispy and lightly brown. Add the bone broth, then scrape the bottom of the pot to remove any stuck brown bits.

2. Stir in the cabbage and bay leaf, then cover with parchment round paper before you put the lid on top and then set the sealing valve to "sealing". Choose "manual" and then set cooking time at 4 minutes.

3. Once the cooking time has been reached, simply press the "keep warm/cancel", and then release the pressure before uncovering the pot and removing the parchment paper.

4. Press "sauté" again and add the nutmeg and coconut oil to boil. Simmer for 5 minutes before turning off the instant pot. Stir in the parsley flakes before serving.

Recipe #21: Fried Teriyaki Chicken Wings

(Total time: 30 minutes, serving: 10-20)
Ingredients:
- 1/3 cup of lemon juice,
- ¼ cup of soy sauce,
- ¼ cup of vegetable oil,
- 3 tablespoons of chili sauce,
- A clove of finely chopped garlic,
- ¼ teaspoon of pepper,
- ¼ teaspoon of celery seed,
- A dash of mustard, and
- 3 pounds (15-20) chicken wings

Directions

1. Prepare the marinade by combining the lemon juice with soy sauce, chili sauce, oil, celery, garlic, pepper, and mustard. Stir very well and set aside.
2. Cut the chicken wings at the joint and remove the tips, then place the chickens in a dish.
3. Pour the marinade over chicken, and then refrigerate overnight, then drain before placing on broiler tray. Choose the "broil" option on the instant pot and set timer at 20 minutes. Once boiling is done, make sure you check the chicken for doneness before transferring them unto the plate.

Recipe #22: Pork Roast With Mushroom Gravy

(Total time: 35 minutes, serving: 2-4)

Ingredients:
- 2 lbs.
- 1 teaspoon of salt,
- ½ a teaspoon of black pepper,
- 4 cups of cauliflower,
- 1 medium onion (chopped),
- 4 cloves of garlic,
- 2 ribs of celery,
- 8 ounces of sliced Portabella mushrooms,
- 2 tablespoons of organic coconut oil and
- 2 cups of clean water.

Directions

1. Place the cauliflower alongside the onion, garlic, celery and water in the bottom of the instant pot. Top up with the pork and season with the salt and pepper.

2. Set the instant pot at boil option and cook at high pressure for 15 minutes after closing the pot and after sealing the valves.

3. Prepare the gravy while the pork is being prepared. Transfer the cooked veggies to the blender and blend smoothly.

4. Cook the mushroom along with the veggies in the instant cooker for 5 minutes (sauté option must be selected). Then serve the mushroom gravy on top of the Pork

Recipe #23: The Fish Batter With "Newcastle" Brown Ale

(Total time: 35 minutes, serving: 4)
Ingredients:
- ½ a teaspoon of garlic powder,
- ½ teaspoon of ground cinnamon,
- 1 qt. of vegetable oil for deep frying,
- ½ a cup of flour,
- ½ a cup of cornmeal,
- 1 teaspoon of garlic salt,
- 1 lb. of cod fillets (cut in pieces),
- 1 cup of brown ale (Newcastle brown ale).

Directions
1. Fry the vegetable oil inside the instant pot for 5 minutes, then whisk together the ingredients inside a large bowl and mix in your until there are no lumps in the batter. Dip the fish cod inside the batter before you place them carefully in the instant pot.
2. Choose the "cook" option and high pressure. Set the timer at 25 minutes and wait until the cod become crispy and brown, especially at the sides.

Recipe #24: The Instant Pot Paleo Egg Roll Soup

(Total time: 40 minutes, serving: 4)

Ingredients:
- 1 teaspoon of olive , ghee or avocado oil,
- 1 lb. of ground organic pork,
- 1 diced large onion,
- 32 ounces (4 cups) of chicken or beef broth,
- ½ chopped head of cabbage,
- 2 cups of shredded carrots,
- 1 teaspoon of garlic powder,
- 1 teaspoon of onion powder,
- 1 teaspoon of sea salt,
- 1 teaspoon of ground ginger,
- 2/3 of a cup of coconut aminos, and
- 2 tablespoons of tapioca starch.

Directions

1. Brown the ground pork inside the instant pot with the oil, and onion. Cook until it is no longer pink (this should take 5 minutes).

2. Add the remaining ingredients and coo further for 20 minutes at high pressure, and once cooking is done, use the quick release option to release the pressure.

3. Remove the lid of the instant pot and serve immediately.

Recipe #25: The Instant Pot Fall Harvest Pork Soup (French Onion Soup)

(Total time: 1 hour 20 minutes, servings: 8)
Ingredients:
- 2 lbs. of boneless pork shoulder,
- 1 can of Campbell condensed French onion soup,
- ½ cup of apple cider,
- 3 large, cut Granny Smith apples,
- 3 cups of seeded, peeled and squash butternut,
- 2 medium peeled and cut parsnips,
- ½ teaspoon of dried and crushed thyme leaves.

Directions

1. Turn on the instant pot and set the timer at 35 minutes. Choose the "soup" option, and press high pressure.

2. Gently stir the pork, apples, cider, parsnips, soup, and thyme inside 5 quarts of water and add to the instant pot. Cover the mix and cook until the pork becomes tender. Press the release once the cooking is done and shred the pork before serving.

Recipe #26: The Sicilian Stuffed Artichoke

(Total time: 45 minutes, servings: 4)

Ingredients:

- 4 big artichokes,
- 4 garlic cloves,
- 2 tablespoons of olive oil,
- 1 fresh lemon (cut into wedges),
- 1 pinch of salt, and
- 8 ounces of thinly sliced Romano cheese.

Directions

1. Remove the stems and tops of the artichokes, then wiggle them back and forth with your thumbs in order to open the leaves. Gently snap off and remove the outer tougher leaves.

2. Place the lemon wedges inside a bowl of water to soak the artichokes (soak the artichokes for about 30 minutes).

Remove the artichokes from the water and shake off excess water from them. Insert the sliced Romano cheese in-between the artichoke leaves and then place a garlic clove in the center of each artichoke.

3. Place the artichoke inside the instant pot and choose "boil" option. Set the timer at 30 minutes at high pressure then place the lid and make sure the valves are seal. Let the instant pot release the pressure naturally once the cooking is done.

Recipe #27: The Steamed Artichoke

(Total time: 30 minutes, serving: 2)

Ingredients:
- 2 large, and whole artichokes,
- 1 garlic clove,
- 1 tablespoon of lemon juice, and
- 1 bay leaf

Directions

1. Cut and discard the stem of artichoke, and ensure the bottom of the artichokes are flat. Likewise, cut the top 1 inch of the artichokes and discard, and the thorny end of each artichoke leaves must be snipped with a scissors, and disposed.

2. Fill up the bottom of the instant pot with water, and add all the ingredients before adding the artichokes.

3. Place the artichoke inside the instant pot and choose "boil" option. Set the timer at 20 minutes at high pressure then place the lid and make sure the valves are seal. Let the instant pot release the pressure naturally once the cooking is done.

Recipe #28: Instant Pot Shredded Chicken

(Total time: 25 minutes, serving: 2-3)

Ingredients:

- 4 lbs. of chicken breast,
- ½ cup of water (or chicken broth),
- 1 teaspoon of salt, and
- ½ a teaspoon of black pepper.

Directions

1. Add all your ingredients into the instant pot, and cover with the lid before you close the pressure valve. Then set the time at 20 minutes at high pressure.

2. Once the cooking time has been completed, simply turn the instant pot's valve from sealing to venting for a quick release of pressure hence the steam will escape and you will be able to open the lid sooner.

3. Place the chicken on the cutting board and make use of forks to shred.

4. Store the chicken inside air-tight container alongside the cooking liquid to keep the meat moist.

Recipe #29: The Family-Friendly Amish Chicken And Corn Soup

(Total time: 30 minutes, serving: 6)

Ingredients:
- 2 quarts of chicken stock or broth,
- ¼ cup of coarsely chopped onion
- ½ of stewing hen or fowl,
- ½ cup of coarsely chopped carrot,
- ½ cup of coarsely chopped celery,
- 1 teaspoon of saffron threads,
- ¾ of a cup of corn kernels,
- 1 teaspoon of chopped parsley (fresh),
- 1 cup of cooked egg noodles

Directions

1. Combine the stewing hen with the chicken stock, onion, carrot, celery, and saffron threads, and then bring to simmer inside the instant pot for 10 minutes at high pressure.
2. Remove the stewing hen mix and let it cool a bit, then separate the meat from the bone and cut into nice pieces. With the aid of a fine sieve, strain the saffron broth, and add the celery, corn, parsley and cooked noodles to your broth and return to instant pot and cover with the lid before you close the pressure valve. Then set the time at 10 minutes at high pressure again.
3. Serve immediately.

Recipe #30: The Ground Beef Chili

(Total time: 35 minutes, serving: 10)

Ingredients:
- 2lbs. ground beef,
- 2 tablespoons of olive oil,
- 2 diced red onions,
- 10 minced garlic cloves,
- 8 chopped carrots,
- 5 stalks of chopped celery,
- 2 chopped bell peppers,
- 1-2 minced jalapenos (remove the ribs and seeds),
- 2 teaspoons of chili powder,
- 1 tablespoon of cumin,
- 1 tablespoon of oregano,
- 2 tablespoon of salt,
- 1 teaspoon of black pepper, and
- ¼ of a teaspoon of cayenne.

Directions

4. Press the "sauté" button on the instant pot before adding the oil, garlic and onions. Sauté for a minute and add the ground beef and cook further until it becomes brown.
5. Add the other ingredients to the pot, and cover to lock the grid.
6. Simply press the "Keep warm/cancel" button, and then press the "bean/chili" button to tart the pressure cooking. This will be automatically set at 30 minutes (make sure you have closed the steam valve before cooking).
7. Once the chili has been prepared, the instant pot will switch automatically to the "Keep warm" mode. Do not use the

quick release option, after cooking, simply allow the pressure to release itself naturally.

8. Garnish the meal with cilantro or sour cream.

Recipe #31: The Japanese Style Deep-Fried Shrimp

(Total time: 25 minutes, serving: 4)
Ingredients:
- 1 lb. of medium size shrimps (de-veined),
- ½ a teaspoon of salt,
- ½ a teaspoon of ground black pepper,
- ½ a teaspoon of garlic powder,
- 1 cup of all-purpose flour,
- 1 teaspoon of paprika,
- 2 large eggs (beaten),
- 1 cup of panko crumbs,
- 1 quart of olive oil.

Directions

1. Prepare the shrimp by removing unwanted items and then wash in water and leave for 3 minutes to dry.

2. Press the "sauté" button on the instant pot, and add the oil alongside other ingredients to the pot. Stir fry the mix for about 15 minutes and serve immediately.

Recipe #32: Instant Pot Cooker Italian Beef

(Total time: 2 hours 10 minutes, servings 2-4)
Ingredients:
- 3 lb. of organic chuck roast,
- 6 cloves of garlic,
- 2 teaspoons of garlic powder,
- 1 teaspoon of onion powder,
- ½ a teaspoon of ground ginger,
- 1 teaspoon of oregano,
- 1 teaspoon of basil,
- 1 teaspoon of marjoram,
- 1 teaspoon of sea salt,
- 1 cup of beef broth, and
- ¼ of a cup of apple cider vinegar.

Directions

1. With the aid of a sharp knife simply cut some slits into the roast and then stuff them with garlic cloves.

2. Get a bowl and inside, simply whisk the organic powder with the onion, oregano, basil, ground ginger, marjoram, and salt and combine them well. Rub the seasoning blends on all sides of the roast, and place it inside the instant pot.

3. Pour the beef broth and apple cider vinegar into the pot before sealing the lid and ensure that the valve is closed.

4. Press the manual button and set cooking time at 90 minutes. Once the cooking is completed, simply allow the natural release to offload the pressure.

5. Remove the beef from the instant pot and shred with a fork.

Recipe #33: The Instant Pot Coconut Orange Rice Pudding

(Total time: 26 minutes, serving: 4)

Ingredients:

- 2 cups of unsweetened almond milk (vanilla flavored and divided),
- 1 cup of orange juice,
- 1 cup of Arborio rice,
- ¼ teaspoon of salt,
- 1 lightly beaten egg,
- 1 teaspoon of orange extract,
- 1/3 of a cup of coconut, and
- 1 teaspoon of grated orange zest.

Directions

1. Combine ¾ of almond milk with the rice, orange juice, and salt inside the pressure cooker of the instant pot. Seal the pressure cooker and select "manual" setting with high pressure, then set the timer at 4 minutes.

2. Let the pressure of the instant pot releases itself naturally (this should take about 10 minutes), and any remaining pressure can be released with the quick-release valve.

3. Whisk the remaining milk, with the egg, and orange extract, inside a small bowl. Add half of the cooked rice and stir the mix until they are all combined well. Pour the mix into the instant pot, and select the "sauté" option, add the coconut and orange zest and cook further for 2 minutes until the egg become set.

4. Serve immediately.

Recipe #34: The Chicken And Veggie Miso Soup

(Total time: 1 hour 7 minutes, servings: 7)

Ingredients:
- 1-2 tablespoons of grapeseed oil,
- 5 carrots (chopped),
- 2 diced leeks,
- 5 ounces of shiitake mushrooms (sliced),
- 1 large onion (diced),
- 2 lbs. of skinless and boneless chicken thighs,
- ½ a teaspoon of salt and ground black pepper,
- 8 cups of chicken broth,
- ½ a cup of miso paste,
- 8 cloves of minced garlic,
- 1 tablespoon of soy sauce,
- 1 piece (2 inch) grated ginger root,
- 1 dash of sriracha. sauce
- ½ of a head of Napa cabbage (torn it to pieces),
- 1 head of a baby bok choy

Directions

1. Pour the grapeseed oil into the instant pot cooker, then add the carrots, leeks, shiitake mushrooms and onion. Select "sauté" setting and cook for 5 minutes.

2. Get a bowl and inside, season the chicken with salt and pepper, then add to the cooker and pour the chicken broth. Seal and cook after choosing the "soup" setting, and 7 minutes cooking time. Release the pressure manually after 10 minutes, then cover the vent with a dish towel before using the quick-release method.

3. Remove the chicken and shred with the aid of a fork, on a cutting board. Return the chicken to the cooker and add the

miso paste, alongside the soy sauce, garlic, ginger and sriracha sauce. Cook further and stir while switching to "sauté" setting, until the miso pastes has dissolve completely (this should take some 5 minutes). Stir in your cabbage and the bok choy and cook further for 5 minutes until the whole recipe softens.

Recipe #35: Artichokes With Sautéed Navy Beans

(Total time: 25 minutes, serving: 4)

Ingredients:

- 1 can of marinated artichoke hearts (quartered and drained),
- 6 tablespoons of olive oil,
- 2 minced garlic cloves,
- ½ teaspoon of freshly ground black pepper,
- ½ a teaspoon of salt , for added taste,
- ½ a teaspoon of ground red pepper,
- 1 can (15 ounces) of rinsed and drained navy beans,
- ¼ of a cup of grated Romano cheese

Directions

1. Heat olive oil inside the instant pot for about 5 minutes, and stir in the red pepper and garlic. Mix in the beans and continue cooking until it becomes crispy. Mix in your artichoke hearts and then cook further for about 2 minutes before seasoning with the black pepper.

2. Top up with Romano cheese before serving.

Recipe #36: The Instant Pot Baked Beef Soup

(Total time: 60 minutes, serving: 8)
Ingredients:
- 1 cup of water,
- 3 tablespoons of tapioca,
- 2 tablespoons of sugar (preferably brown),
- ½ a teaspoon of pepper,
- 1 ½ teaspoons of salt,
- ½ a teaspoon of pepper,
- 2 lbs. of stew meat (cut into an inch cubes),
- 4 large carrots (diced into an inch chunks),
- 2 celery ribs (cut into ¾ chunks),
- 1 large onion cut into smaller chunks, and
- A sliced bread.

Directions

1. Get a large bowl and combine the water with, tapioca, salt, sugar and pepper. Add the remaining ingredients and mix properly.

2. Pour the mix into the instant pot and secure the lid and the valves before setting the cooking time at 30 minutes and choose "soup" option.

3. The vegetables should be tender and the soup becomes bubbly by the time the cooking has been completed. Let the pressure eases off naturally (this should take about 10 minutes).

Recipe #37: The Country Chicken Stew

(Total time: 40minutes, serving: 4)

Ingredients:
- 2 slices of diced bacon,
- A medium sliced onion,
- 2 medium sliced carrots,
- 1 condensed cream of chicken soup,
- 1 cup of frozen beans,
- 2 chunks of drained chicken breast in water,
- A can of soup water
- ½ teaspoon of crushed dried oregano leaves,
- 2 tablespoons of fresh parsley (chopped).

Directions

1. Cook the bacon inside the instant pot with a little water, for 10 minutes at high pressure until it becomes crispy.

2. Remove the bacon and dry on paper towel. Add the onion inside the pot, and stir occasionally. Stir in the soup, oregano, carrots, and then heat until the mix boils. Add the bacon into the pot again, cover to cook for about 15 minutes.

3. Stir in your beans, then cover and cook for about 10 minutes until the vegetable becomes tender. Stir in your parsley, bacon and chicken, then stir until the mixture becomes hot and bubbling.

Recipe #38: The Tasty Instant Pot Aromatic Lamp Chops

(Total time: 60 minutes, serving: 5)
Ingredients:
- 15 lamb loin chops (3 ounces and 1-inch thick each),
- 1 tablespoon of fresh lemon juice,
- 2 slice garlic cloves,
- 1 tablespoon of soy sauce,
- 1 teaspoon of garlic powder (for added taste),
- 2 tablespoons of olive oil,
- 1 pinch of chili powder,
- ¼ of chopped fresh cilantro,
- 2 tablespoons of brown sugar,
- 2 lime wedges, and
- 1 teaspoon of freshly ground pepper (for added taste).

Directions

1. Place the lambs inside a roasting pan, before seasoning with garlic powder, garlic, sugar, chili powder, salt, sugar, and pepper. Simply drizzle the mix with the lime juice alongside the soy sauce, and olive oil before covering and refrigerating overnight.
2. Thaw for 5 minutes, then add olive oil inside the instant pot. Add the ingredients (except the lemon squeeze and lime juice). Choose "sauté" and then close with the lid before setting the time at 30 minutes). Once it is done, simply garnish by sprinkling cilantro and squeeze the lemon and lime juices over the top before serving.

Recipe #39: The Instant Pot Vegetarian Curry Soup

(Total time: 60 minutes, serving: 8)

Ingredients:
- 3 teaspoons of vegetable oil,
- 3 ½ cups of vegetable broth,
- 1 coarsely chopped onion,
- 4 cups of water,
- 2 thinly sliced shallots,
- 2 optional tablespoons of vegetarian fish sauce,
- 2 cloves chopped garlic,
- 2 tablespoons of red pepper flakes,
- 2-inch thinly sliced fresh ginger root,
- 1 bay leaf,
- 1 stalk of lemon grass (cut into 2-inch pieces),
- 2 kaffir lime leaves,
- 3 tablespoons of curry powder,
- 1 coarsely chopped green pepper,
- 1 can of coconut milk,
- 2 peeled and sliced carrots,
- 2 cups of fresh bean sprouts (for garnishing),
- 8 sliced mushrooms,
- 8 sprigs of chopped cilantro (for garnishing),
- 1 lb. of pound tofu (cut into bit sizes).

Directions
1. Sauté the onion and shallots inside the sauce pan for 5 minutes until they become translucent and soft. Stir in your

garlic, curry powder, lemon grass and ginger. Cook the mix for about 5 minutes, before stirring in the green pepper, mushrooms, carrots and tofu.

2. Pour the vegetable stock and water before seasoning with fish sauce and red pepper flakes. Bring the mix to boil before stirring in coconut milk.

3. Return the soup to boiling before reducing the heat to very low, to simmer- this should take about 20 minutes . Garnish the bowl with cilantro and bean sprouts.

Recipe #40: Instant Pot Stir Fries With Beef And Green Beans

(Total time: 30 minutes, serving: 4)
Ingredients:
- 1 clove minced garlic,
- 2 ½ tablespoons of vegetable oil,
- ¼ of a teaspoon of ground black pepper,
- ½ thinly sliced onion,
- 1 teaspoon of corn starch,
- 2 cups of fresh green beans (trimmed and washed),
- 1 teaspoon of vegetable oil,
- ¼ cup of chicken broth,
- 1 lb. of thinly sliced Sirloin tips, and
- 1 teaspoon of soy sauce.

Directions

1. Get a large mixing bowl and inside combine the black pepper with the garlic, cornstarch, and the vegetable oil. Add the beef and mix well. Then add the meat before cooking and stirring them for about 2 minutes inside the instant pot, until the beef has begun turning brown. Transfer the beef into a large bowl and then set it aside.

2. Add the onion and stir fry until it turns tender. Mix in the green beans and the broth, then cover and simmer for about 5 minutes until the beans have become crispy tender. Stir in your soy sauce plus the beef and cook while stirring continuously for about 2 minutes until the mix has been heated through.

3. Let the instant pot release the pressure once cooking is completed and serve immediately.

Recipe #41: The Traditional Instant Pot Pho Ga Soup

(Total time: 30 minutes, serving: 5)
Ingredients:
- 1 tablespoon of vegetable oil,
- 2 shredded and cooked chicken breasts,
- 1 small chopped yellow onion,
- 4 green chopped onions,
- 1 pack baby bella mushroom (chopped),
- 1/3 of a cup of chopped fresh Cilantro,
- 4 minced garlic cloves,
- 2 cups of bean sprouts,
- 7 teaspoons of chicken bouillon
- 8 cups of water,
- 1 lime (sliced into wedges),
- 1 pack of rice stick noodles (about 7 ounces), and
- 1 dash of Sriracha hot sauce.

Directions
1. Sauté the onions, alongside the mushroom, and garlic and the veggies for about 10 minutes, until they become tender, inside the instant pot.
2. Add the water, alongside the rice noodles, as well as chicken bouillon, to the onion mix, and bring the mix to boil.
3. Mix the shredded chicken with the Cilantro, and green onions into the soup. Let the mix simmer for about 5 minutes, before transferring the soup inside the serving bowls. Top up with bean sprouts plus a squeeze of lemon juice as well as Sriracha sauce. And sauté for about 5 minutes, before the pressure cooker turns off.

4. Serve immediately.

Recipe #42: Crab Meat With Asparagus Soup

(Total time: 35 minutes, serving: 6)

Ingredients:

- 1 can (10 ounce) of drained Asparagus tips,
- 1 cup of fresh spinach (chopped),
- 2 cans of crab eat (6 ounce, drained and flaked),
- 1 cup of firm tofu (diced),
- 2 tablespoons of fish sauce,
- 2 tablespoons of dried oregano,
- 1 tablespoon of oyster sauce, and
- 1 crushed clove garlic.

Directions

1. Turn on the instant pot and inside combine the asparagus with the spinach, tofu, crab meat, oregano, fish sauce, and garlic. Make sure you fill the crockpot with water until 2 inches full.
2. Cover the mix and cook for 25 minutes on high pressure while the valves are tight sealed and the pot is covered. Make sure the spinach has cooked properly and you can smell the flavor.
3. Transfer into the serving bowl.

Recipe #43: Scintillating Fried Squid With Pineapple

(Total time: 25 minutes, serving: 4)
Ingredients:
- 4 stalks of celery (cut into 2-inch pieces),
- 2 tablespoons of vegetable oil,
- 3 cloves of minced garlic,
- 3 tablespoons of fish sauce,
- 1 large onion (cut into wedges),
- 1 teaspoon of brown sugar,
- 2 lbs. of squid (cleaned and sliced into ½ inch rings),
- 1/2 teaspoon of ground black pepper

Directions

1. Add the vegetable oil to the instant pot and press the "sauté" button, then sauté the garlic, until the garlic turns golden brown. Add the onion and stir-fry for about 60 seconds, then add the squid and cook further for 15 minutes until the squid turns white. Add the remaining ingredients and stir fry further for 2 minutes.

2. Once the cooking time is completed, simply allow the recipes to cool before serving.

Recipe #44: Instant Pot Vietnamese Eggplant With Spicy Sauce

(Total time: 30 minutes, serving: 2)

Ingredients:
- 1 tablespoon of freshly chopped basil,
- 3 tablespoons of divided vegetable oil,
- 1 sliced white eggplant,
- 1 teaspoon of minced ginger (fresh),
- 3 tablespoons of minced lemon grass,
- 1 teaspoon of minced fresh ginger,
- 1 tablespoon of crushed garlic,
- 1 tablespoon of oyster sauce ,
- 1 tablespoon of green onion (chopped),
- 1 teaspoon of white sugar.

Directions

1. Heat 1 teaspoon of vegetable oil at medium heat inside the instant pot. Add your eggplant and then cook until it becomes golden brown and soft (cook each side for about 4 minutes but make sure it does not get mushy).

2. Get a bowl and inside mix together, the remaining 2 tablespoons of vegetable oil, with the green onion, garlic, lemon grass, Ginger, red Chile, and basil. Pour this mix over the eggplant inside the instant pot and cook until the green onion has wilted (this should take 3 minutes). Stir in your oyster sauce and sugar and then cook until the flavor have combined very well – this should take some 3 minutes.

3. Release the sealed valves slowly before opening the instant pot.

Recipe #45: The Instant Pot Chickpea Curry

(Total time: 35 minutes, serving: 8)

Ingredients:
- 2 tablespoons of vegetable oil,
- 2 minced average onions,
- 2 cloves of minced garlic,
- 2 tablespoons of fresh finely chopped fresh ginger root,
- 6 whole cloves,
- 2 sticks of crushed cinnamon ,
- 1 teaspoon of ground cumin,
- 1 teaspoon of ground coriander,
- ½ teaspoon of salt,
- ½ teaspoon of Cayenne pepper,
- 1 teaspoon of ground turmeric,
- 2 cans of garbanzo beans,
- 1 cup of fresh chopped cilantro

Directions
1. Open the instant pot and set it at "sauté". Heat the oil in the frying pan over and fry the onions until tender. Stir all other ingredients inside the oil and cook for about a minute while stirring constantly.
2. Mix the beans along with the liquid, and continue to cook the mix until all ingredients are blended (20 minutes).
3. Stir in the Cilantro once the cooking time is completed and you have released the valve.
4. Serve immediately.

Recipe #46: Artichoke Salsa

(Total time: 15 minutes, serving: 5)

Ingredients:

- 1 jar (6.5 ounce) of drained and chopped, marinated artichoke hearts,
- 1 tablespoon of chopped garlic,
- 2 tablespoons of chopped fresh basil,
- ½ teaspoon each of salt and pepper (for added taste),
- 2 tablespoons of chopped red onion, and
- ¼ of a cup of chopped black olives.

Directions

1. Get a medium size bowl and inside, mix all the ingredient and serve chilled under room temperature with Tortilla chip
2. To keep it warm, simply pour the recipe inside the instant pot and press "warm" and set the timer at 10 minutes and shut the valve after closing the lid.

Recipe #47: The Instant Pot Alfredo Sauce With Artichoke

(Total time: 30 minutes, serving: 5)
Ingredients:
- 1 can (15 ounce) of artichoke hearts soaked in water,
- 1 chopped large onion,
- 1 cup of fresh sliced mushrooms,
- ½ a cup of chopped fresh basil,
- ½ a cup of whole milk,
- 2 tablespoons of all-purpose flour.

Directions

1. Chop the artichoke hearts and then place them in the large pan of the instant pot, then thicken them with milk and flour and mix until desired thickness and consistency are met. Press the "cook" button on the pan.

2. Add the remaining ingredients, add the lid, and then shut the valve. Cook for about 10 minutes making sure the veggies are firm and tasty. Pour the cooked recipe in a bowl.

3. Cook enough of your favorite spaghetti brand inside the hot pot, and rinse before topping up with the artichoke mix (This should take about 10 minutes).

4. Serve immediately.

Recipe #48: The 15-Minute Barbecue Chicken Soup

(Total time: 20 minutes serves: 4)

Ingredients:

- 2 tablespoons of extra virgin olive oil,
- 1.5 cups of chicken broth,
- ½ cup f barbecue sauce,
- 1 tablespoon of minced garlic,
- ½ a teaspoon of Kosher salt,
- 1 can of drained Mexican corn,
- 2 large cooked and shredded chicken breasts
- ¼ teaspoon of black pepper,
- ¼ teaspoon of garlic salt, and
- ¼ cup of fresh and chopped cilantro leaves

Directions

1. Add all your ingredients into the instant pot, and cover with the lid before you close the pressure valve. Then set the time at 14 minutes at high pressure.

2. Once the cooking time has been completed, simply turn the instant pot's valve off and pour soup in a serving bowl.

Recipe #49: The Instant Pot Salsa Chicken

(Total time: 40 minutes, serving)
Ingredients:
- 1 lb. of frozen , skinless and boneless chicken breasts (halved),
- ½ a cup of salsa,
- 1 (an ounce) pack of taco seasoning mix, and
- ½ a cup of low sodium chicken broth.

Directions

1. Place the chicken breasts inside the instant pot, then spray the taco seasoning to the sides of the chicken. Pour the salsa and chicken broth on the top.

2. Cover the pot with the lid, and choose the poultry setting before setting the timer at 15 minutes. Once the cooking has ended, simply allow the pressure to release itself naturally (this make take up to 20 minutes). Shred the cooked chicken immediately before serving.

Recipe #50: Instant Pot Rosemary Lemon Chicken

(Total time: 54 minutes, serving: 4)

Ingredients:
- 6 breast halves of chicken (with bones),
- ¾ of a whole lemon (peeled and sliced into rounds),
- ½ of a whole orange (peeled and sliced into rounds),
- 3 cloves of roasted garlic,
- ½ teaspoon each of salt and ground pepper,
- 1 ½ tablespoons of olive oil,
- 1 ½ teaspoons of agave syrup,
- 1 splash of red wine,
- 1 splash of white wine,
- ¼ cup of water,
- 2 sprigs of fresh rosemary (stemmed).

Directions

1. Place the chicken inside the instant pot then toss in the rounds of lemon, orange, and garlic, before seasoning with salt and pepper. Drizzle the olive oil on the top, alongside the agave. Add the red and white wines, then cover with water. Add the rosemary before you put the cover lid and lock the cooker in place.
2. Select the "meat and stew" settings at high pressure and then set the timer at 14 minutes. Cook the chicken until it is no longer pink at the bones and allow the instant pot to release its pressure naturally (this should take about 20 minutes).
3. Serve immediately.

Recipe #51: Arctic Char With A Bed Of Kale

(Total time: 30 minutes, servings: 3)

Ingredients

- A teaspoon of extra virgin olive oil,
- A thinly sliced large shallot,
- A cup of chicken broth
- ¼ cup of water,
- 1 pound of chopped kale,
- A pound of skinned arctic char,
- ¼ teaspoon of salt,
- ¼ teaspoon of freshly ground pepper,
- ¼ cup of sour cream (with zero or reduced fat),
- 2 teaspoons of horseradish,
- A tablespoon of fresh dill and
- 4 lemon wedges for garnishing.

Direction

1. Set your instant pot at "sauté", at high pressure, and set timer at 10 minutes, then cook shallot until soften. Add the kale and cook for 5 minutes extra, until tender. Sprinkle the fish with salt and pepper and

2. Place on the kale, cover and cook for about 7 minutes. Meanwhile, add the sour cream, dill and horseradish inside a bowl then serve with the fish, kale and the sauce with lemon garnish.

Recipe #52: The Red Snapper Caribbean Recipe

(Total time: 25 minutes, servings: 2)

Ingredients

- A medium chopped onion,
- 2 tablespoons of olive oil,
- ½ cup of chopped red pepper,
- ½ cup of stripped carrots,
- A minced clove garlic,
- ½ cup of dry white wine,
- ½ a pound of red snapper fish fillet,
- 2 tablespoon of non-fat feta cheese,

Direction

1. Turn on the instant pot and set timer at 5 minutes at high pressure, then Heat olive oil. Add the onion, carrots, garlic and red pepper before you sauté for about 10 minutes. Then add the wine before boiling further and pushing the veggies to one side.

2. Arrange the fillets in a single layer at the center of the pan, then cover and cook for about 5 minutes. Add the olives before topping with cheese, then cook with the fish further for 3 minutes until they are firm. Transfer the mix to a serving platter and garnish with pan juices and veggies.

Recipe #53: Instant Pot Mini-Lemon Cheesecakes

(Total time: 18 minutes Servings: 6)
Ingredients
- 6 half-pint mason jars,
- 16 oz. of cream cheese (at room temperature),
- ½ a cup of sugar,
- 1 teaspoon of flour,
- ½ a teaspoon of vanilla,
- ¼ of a cup of sour cream (at room temperature),
- 1 tablespoon of lemon juice,
- 1 lemon zest,
- 3 medium to large eggs,
- 1 jar of lemon curd,
- ½ a cup of raspberries (optional), and
- 1 ½ cups of water.

Direction
1. Get a large mixing bowl, and inside beat the cream cheese with the sugar, and flour, until mix has become creamy and has no lumps. Beat in the vanilla, lemon juice, sour cream, and lemon zest and mix them very well. Beat in an egg at a time, and until well-mixed (do not over-beat the eggs).
2. Fill each of the jar with ¼ of a cup of the batter of cheesecake, and then drop 1 tablespoon of lemon curd on top of the batter. Add an additional ¼ of a cup of cheesecake batter to each jar and on top of the lemon curd before you cover each jar loosely with foil.

3. Add the water to the bottom of the instant pot, and ten place the trivet at the bottom. Arrange 3 of the jars at the bottom of the instant pot, and then stark the remaining 3 jars on top of the bottom three. Secure the instant pot lid and ensure that the vent remains in the pressure cooking point.
4. Set timer at 8 minutes and manually cook. Once the cooking is completed, simply perform a manual pressure release and carefully remove the jars from the instant pot with the aid of a pad or towel. Cool the cheesecakes at room temperature until they are ready to be served.
5. Garnish the cheesecakes with raspberries and additional lemon curds.

Recipe #54: Artichoke In Garlic And Olive Oil Sauce

(Total time: 25 minutes serves: 2)

Ingredients:

- 2 cloves of garlic,
- 1 chopped sprig fresh basil,
- 1 can (18 ounce) of artichoke hearts – quartered and drained,
- 3 tablespoons of butter,
- 2 ½ tablespoons of extra virgin olive oil , and
- 4 ounces of small uncooked seashell pasta.

Direction

1. Lightly salt 2 cups of water and pour it inside the instant pot and press the "boil" option at high pressure, then close the lid and secure the valve, and bring it to boil. Add the seashell pasta, and cook for about 10 minutes until it becomes dense, then drain.

2. Remove the boiled pasta.

3. Heat the olive oil and then melt the butter inside the sauce pan at high pressure (2 minutes), then mix in the garlic basil and artichoke hearts before cooking for 5 minutes, until it becomes heated through. Toss it with the cooked pasta before serving.

Recipe #55: Porridge Served With Cinnamon

This is a delicious fat-burning aid recipe that works best in the morning.

Preparation time: 20 minutes

Servings: 1

Ingredients

- 30g of whole oats,
- 1 cup of water,
- ½ cup of skimmed milk, and
- 5g of Cinnamon.

Direction

1. Measure out the porridge and place in a non-sticky pan, add the milk and water before bringing to boil, turn down the heat low and let it simmer for about 5 minutes. Stir the mix to avoid one part getting cooked and the other not cooked. Sprinkle your cinnamon on top and enjoy.

Recipe #56: Instant Pot Prosciutto Fritters (Polpette Di Patate Fritte)

(Total time: 20 minutes, Servings: 4)

Ingredients:

- 2 slices of chopped Prosciutto,
- ¼ of a cup of al purpose flour,
- ½ teaspoons each of ground black pepper and salt,
- 1 large egg, and
- 1 1/4 of a cup of extra virgin olive oil

Direction:

1. Get a medium bowl and inside, place the flour, egg and the ham, then mix very well. Season the mix with the salt and pepper, before forming the mix into fritters.

2. Heat oil inside the sauce pan, then fry the fritters until they turn golden in color (this should take about 5 minutes on both sides).

3. Press the quick release once frying is completed, then serve.

Recipe #57: Sautéed Navy Beans Artichoke

(Total time 20 minutes: serves: 4)

Ingredients:

- 1 can of marinated artichoke hearts (quartered and drained),
- 6 tablespoons of olive oil,
- 2 minced garlic cloves,
- ½ teaspoon of freshly ground black pepper,
- ½ a teaspoon of salt , for added taste,
- ½ a teaspoon of ground red pepper,
- 1 can (15 ounces) of rinsed and drained navy beans,
- ¼ of a cup of grated Romano cheese

Direction

1. Open the instant pot and add the oil, set the option at "sauté", and set timer at 5 minutes at high pressure. Close the lid heat olive oil inside the instant pot and stir in the red pepper and garlic.

2. Mix in the beans and continue cooking until it becomes crispy. Mix in your artichoke hearts and then cook further for about 2 minutes before seasoning with the black pepper. Top up with Romano cheese before serving

Recipe #58: Delicious Egg Scrambles With Spinach

(Total time: 25 minutes, serving: 3)
Ingredients:
- 1 chopped onion,
- 3 tbsp. of peanut oil,
- A pound of lean ground beef,
- A pound of drained, chopped spinach,
- 1 tsp. of Tabasco sauce,
- 4 lightly beaten eggs, and
- 4 tablespoons of grated parmesan cheese.

Direction:
1. Heat the peanut oil inside the Instant pot for 5 minutes; add the onion and sauté until soft. Add the beef and with a fork, break the beef in pieces.
2. Cook the meat for 10 minutes and add the spinach, then mix well and cook further for 3 minutes before adding salt. Mix the egg with the Tabasco, and pour the mix over the beef mix, before cooking and stir until the eggs are set. Remove from instant pot by pressing the pressure release.
3. Transfer the mix to a platter and sprinkle the parmesan.

Recipe #59: Garlic Sautéed Artichoke

(Total time: 30 minutes, Servings: 4)

Ingredients:
- 2 large artichokes (about 1 lb. each),
- 3 cloves of chopped garlic,
- 2 tablespoons of butter.

Direction

1. Rinse the artichoke under cold water, then make use of a sharp knife to cut the top 1/3 part while trimming the stem to about an inch. Remove the smaller leaves located around the base, and then make use of a scissors to remove the remaining leaf tips. Cut each of the artichokes into halves from bottom to top, and make use of a spoon to scrape the hairy choke. Rinse once again to remove any leftover hairs.

2. Open the instant pot, set the timer at 5 minutes and choose "sauté" option, at high pressure. Pour the butter inside, melt the butter, before adding the garlic and then sauté for about a minute further in order to flavor the butter. Arrange the artichokes with the cut side facing down in the instant pot. Sautee the mix for about 10 minutes until they turn lightly brown, and pour ¼ of a cup of water, before covering.

3. Let the mix steam for about 10 minutes until artichoke becomes tender.

4. Once the final cooking time has been completed, simply release the valve and pour the meal in a serving bowl.

Recipe #60: The Mediterranean Fried Cabbage Served With Bacon And Onion

(Total time: 35 minutes, serving:2)

Ingredients:

- 7 thin slices of bacon,
- 2 tbsp. of butter,
- A small thinly sliced onion,
- A small cabbage head (cut into half),
- 2 tbsp. of cider vinegar,
- 1 optional bay leaf, and
- A cup of water.

Direction:

1. Cut the bacon into 1-inch pieces and place them in the instant pot and cook until they are ready to be turned, then add the butter and onion, and then cook until slightly brown. Add the cabbage and bay leaf, and add sufficient water to cover. This should take 10 minutes

2. Allow the mix to steam, stir and then add some water to loosen brown bits in the pan. Cook for 20 minutes, until it has attained the right tenderness. Add the vinegar and stir for 5 minutes, then sprinkle the black pepper and serve immediately.

Recipe #61: The Steamed-Cooked Artichoke

(Preparation time: 30 minutes, serving: 2)

Ingredients:
- 2 large, and whole artichokes,
- 1 garlic clove,
- 1 tablespoon of lemon juice, and
- 1 bay leaf

Direction
1. Cut and discard the stem of artichoke, and ensure the bottom of the artichokes are flat. Likewise, cut the top 1 inch of the artichokes and discard, and the thorny end of each artichoke leaves must be snipped with a scissors, and disposed.
2. Fill up the bottom of instant pot with water, and add all the ingredients.
3. Place the artichokes inside the Instant pot and make sure the artichokes rest on their flattened bottoms.
4. Cover the pot, then set timer at 20 minutes at high pressure before closing the lid and secure the valve. Bring the water to boil. Cook the artichoke until it become easy to pull their leaves away. This should take less than 30 minutes.

Recipe #62: Creamy Toasted Garlic Mushrooms

(Total time: 20 minutes, serving: 2-3)

Ingredients;

- 15g of Flora pro-active margarine,
- 1 medium peeled garlic clove,
- 100g of wiped and peeled mushroom,
- Philadelphia soft cream cheese,
- 1 medium sliced Warburton bread (sliced), fresh parsley for garnish, and
- 1 pinch of salt and pepper for taste.

Direction:

1. Place half of the margarine into the instant pot, and then set instant pot at high pressure and 1 minute. Choose "sauté" option and close the lid. Add your garlic, and then cook the mixture for about 1 minute before adding the sliced mushroom.

2. Cook the mix over a low heat for about 7 minutes. Add your cream cheese and cook further for 3 minutes, and let the cream cheese melt completely into the mushrooms before you season with salt and pepper.

3. Toast your bread and spread the margarine over it, and then cut them into triangles (4), before using the spoon to spread the garlic mushroom over them. Garnish the delicious meal with the fresh parsley and serve immediately.

Recipe #63: The Lentils And Spinach Mix

(Total time: 1 hour, Servings: 2-3)
Ingredients:
- 1 tbsp. of vegetable oil,
- 2 halved and sliced onions,
- 3 cloves of minced garlic,
- ½ cup lentils,
- 2 cups of water,
- 10 ounce , or a pack of frozen spinach
- 1 tsp. of ground cumin,
- 1 tsp. of salt,
- 1 tsp. of freshly ground pepper for some taste, and
- 2 crushed cloves garlic.

Direction:

1. Add the oil into the instant pot, and sauté the onion for 2 minutes until it turns golden, then add the garlic and sauté further for 1 minute. Add lentils and water to the sauce pan, and let the mix boil , then cover an lower the heat and let it simmer for 15 minutes further when the lentils have soften.

2. Cook the spinach in microwave, then add the cooked microwave, salt, and the cumin to the pan containing lentils, then cover and simmer for 10 minutes, then add the pepper before serving.

Recipe #64: Artichoke Tetrazzini

(Total time: 25 minutes, Servings: 4)
Ingredients:
- 1 pack of linguini pasta (8 ounce),
- 1 cup of fresh sliced mushroom,
- ¼ of a cup of chopped onion,
- 2 tablespoon of butter,
- 1/8 teaspoon of dried thyme,
- 2 tablespoons of all-purpose flour,
- 1 can (10.5 ounce), of condensed chicken broth,
- 1 cup of half – and –half cream,
- 1 can (6 ounce) of marinated artichoke hearts,
- ¼ of a cup of grated parmesan cheese.

Direction

1. Open the instant pot, and opt for "boil" option and set timer at 5 minutes and cook the linguini in hot and salted water, over medium heat.

2. Once the cooking of the linguini is completed transfer it to another plate or bowl, then change the instant pot to "sauté" option and sauté the onion with the mushroom, butter, and thyme, for 5 minutes before stirring in the flour. Stir in the chicken broth plus the half and half cream, and take it back to instant pot and choose "boil" option with 10 minutes, and boil until the sauce boils and becomes thicken. Strain the artichokes and stir in the liquid into the sauce before adding the parmesan cheese.

3. Drain the linguini and toss with the sauce. Fold in the artichokes before serving.

Recipe #65: The Vegetarian Cassoulet

(Total time 40 minutes, serving: 1-2)
Ingredients:
- 2 tbsp. of olive oil,
- 1 large onion,
- 2 peeled and sliced carrots,
- 1 pound of dry navy beans (soaked overnight),
- 4 cups of mushroom broth,
- 1 cube of vegetable bouillon,
- 1 small or medium bay leaf,
- 4 sprigs of parsley,
- 1 sprig of fresh rosemary,
- 1 sprig of chopped fresh lemon thyme,
- 1 sprig of fresh savory, and

Direction:

1. Simply heat some oil in the instant pot, then add the onion and carrot inside the oil and stir until they become tender.

2. Combine the ingredients inside a pan and add water, then add to the instant pot cooker. Make sure you tie the rosemary, parsley, thyme, and savory to the pot, cook further for 30 minutes at high pressure, but remove the herbs before serving.

Recipe #66: Coconut Little Kiss (Beijinho De Coco)

(Total time: 40 minutes; **Servings: 10)**
Ingredients:
- 1 can of sweet, condensed milk (14 ounces),
- 1 tablespoon of butter ,
- Some sweetened coconut for decoration,
- Whole cloves for decoration, and
- ¼ cup of sweetened flaked coconut.

Direction

1. Turn on the instant pot, and inside, simply bring the milk and butter to simmer over medium heat. Cook and stir continuously, until the milk volume has been reduced to half and thickened (about 20 minutes). Remove the mix from heat, and stir in the coconut and allow to cool for 3 minutes before you butter the bowl. Chill the mix in refrigerator for about 2 hours.

2. With your oiled or buttered hand, form the milk mix into tablespoon-sized balls before rolling in the coconut flakes. Decorate each beijinho with a stick of clove.

Recipe #67: Chicken With Artichoke

(Total time: 35 minutes, servings: 6)

Ingredients:

- 2 tablespoon of olive oil,
- 1 teaspoon of salt,
- ½ sliced onion,
- 2 cloves of minced garlic,
- 1 lb. of skinless , boneless, chicken breast (cut into halves and 1-inch piece each),
- ½ teaspoon of freshly ground pepper,
- ½ teaspoon of dried basil,
- ½ a teaspoon of dried oregano,
- 1 pack (12 ounce), of Angel hair pasta,
- 1 pack (8 ounce) crumbled feta cheese,
- 1 can (15 ounce) of quartered artichoke hearts(not drained),
- ½ a cup of chicken broth.

Direction

1. Inside the instant pot simply heat olive oil by choosing "sauté" option at high pressure and set the timer at 10 minutes. Add onion and garlic, and stir while cooking for about a minute extra. Add the chicken, then cook and stir for about 5 minutes until the chicken is no longer pink. Stir in the artichoke heart, chicken broth and all other ingredients then cover the skillet and simmer until the chicken is cooked thoroughly (5 minutes). Once the cooking is done simple release the valve before transferring the recipe into a bowl.
2. Get a lightly salted water inside the instant pot and boil for 5 minutes at high pressure, then cook the angel hair pasta in the boiling water while stirring occasionally until it has cooked through . Drain and transfer the pasta unto a platter

and then spoon the chicken mix on top of the pasta. Sprinkle the feta cheese on top before serving.

Recipe #68: The Instant Pot Cheese Cake

(Total time: 3h 48minutes,prp time:30 servings: 8)

Ingredients:
- ¾ of a cup of crushed graham crackers,
- 2 2/3 of a cup of white sugar,
- 1 teaspoon of ground cinnamon,
- 3 tablespoons of melted butter,
- 2/3 of a cup of sour cream,
- 2 large eggs (stored at room temperature),
- 1 zested lemon,
- 1 teaspoon of vanilla extract,
- ¼ of a teaspoon of kosher salt,

For the batter, you need 2 packs (8 ounce) of cream cheese stored at room temperature.

Directions

1. Pulse the Graham crackers, alongside 2 teaspoons of white sugar, and cinnamon, inside the food processor, then pour in the butter, and pulse again until fine crumbs are formed. Pat the crust unto the bottom of 1 inch x 6 inch springform pan and set the pan in the freezer for about 20 minutes.

2. Get a medium stand mixer bowl and mix the cream cheese at low speed until it turns creamy and aerated. Add the remaining 2/3 cup of sugar, plus the salt, and mix further for about 4 minutes. Add the vanilla extra alongside lemon zest before mixing the batter for an extra 1 minute.

3. Crack 1 of the eggs into the batter, then add the remaining eggs. Mix for 60 seconds before stirring in the sour cream. Mix again until the sour cream has disappeared into the batter, then pour the mix into the crust-lined pan, and add cover with aluminum foil.

4. Pour the water unto the bottom of the instant pot, then add the trivet before lowering the filled springform pan slowly into the instant pot. Lock the lid of the instant pot into place.

5. Choose the manual setting and select "high pressure". Set the cooking time at 40 minutes, and allow the pressure to ease itself naturally after the cooking time. Remove the lid and check the edge and center of the cake for doneness (they should jiggle gently when shaken).

6. Transfer your cheese cake into the refrigerator and let it chill for about 2 hours or overnight.

Recipe #69: The Lifesaver Bbq Pressure Chicken Wings

(Total time: 10 minutes, servings: 8-10 wings)

Ingredients:

- 8-10 chicken wings,
- 2 teaspoons of olive oil,
- 4 drops of your favorite chicken wings.

Direction

1. Add your sauce to the chicken wings and make sure you marinate all over them, then pour olive oil inside the sauce pan.

2. Pressure-cook the chicken for 10 minutes inside the olive oil, while the sauce pan is covered.

3. Pat the chicken wings dry, and serve.

Recipe 70: The Instant Pot Deviled Eggs

(Total time: 30 minutes, servings: 12-16)

Ingredients:
- 6-8 eggs,
- 1 cup (250 mls) of cold water,
- 1 tablespoon of extra virgin olive oil,
- 1 teaspoon of Dijon Mustard,
- 1 teaspoon of white vinegar,
- ½ a teaspoon of Sriracha,
- 2 tablespoons of mayonnaise (full fat),
- ½ teaspoon each of ground black pepper and salt

Direction

1. Boil the eggs in the instant pot by placing the water and a steamer basket into the pressure cooker. Then place the eggs into the steamer basket before placing the basket before closing the lid. Set timer at 12 minutes and then press the quick release before opening the lid. Peel the eggs after boiling.

2. Remove the yolk from the white egg by slicing the cooled boiled eggs in halves, and remove the yolks carefully into a mixing bowl. Gently smash the egg yolks with a fork and set the egg whites aside.

3. Make the dressing by adding the mayonnaise to the olive oil, Dijon mustard, white vinegar and Sriracha, and the mix into the smashed egg yolk.

4. Pipe your dressing by placing the dressing inside a Ziploc bag and then cut a small corner with the aid of a scissors, before piping the dressing unto the egg whites.

5. Garnish your eggs by sprinkling the paprika unto the deviled eggs, and then season with the ground pepper and salt

Recipe #71: Instant Pot Korean Ribs

(Total time: 45 minutes, servings: 4)

Ingredients:
- 1 rack (2 lb.) of back black ribs (kalbi marinade),
- 1 peeled and grated Asian pear,
- 1 whole minced garlic (37g),
- 1 minced small or medium onion ,
- ½ a teaspoon of minced ginger,
- 1 teaspoon of freshly ground pepper,
- ½ a cup of light soy sauce,
- 2 tablespoons of honey,
- 2 tablespoons of brown sugar,
- 2 tablespoons of unseasoned rice vinegar,
- 2 tablespoons of sesame oil
- 2 stalks of finely sliced green onions (for garnish),
- 1 tablespoon of toasted sesame seed

Direction

1. Make your Kalbi marinade by cutting the onion and Asian pear into bits, then process the garlic and onion, alongside the Asian pear and ginger inside a food processor. Get a small bowl and inside, mix the soy sauce, with honey, ground black pepper, brown sugar, rice vinegar and sesame oil, then add the mix into the food process to create a paste.

2. Marinate your baby back ribs by removing the outer membrane from the ribs, then place the ribs inside the Kalbi marinade inside a large Ziploc bag. Close the bag partially, then marinate the ribs inside the refrigerator for about 30 minutes.

3. Cook the marinated baby ribs inside the instant pot by pouring everything from the Ziploc bag into the pressure cooker,

then close the lid and set cooking time at 20 minutes (you may reduce the cooking time to 16 minutes if you want it to be more tender and chewy).

4. Turn on the heat and press the release once cooking is done. Brush the sides of the ribs and garnish with green onions and sesame seed before serving.

Recipe #72: The Classic Instant Pot Soy Sauce Eggs

(Total time: 20 minutes; Servings: 4-8)
Ingredients:
- 1 ½ cup of Chinese master stock (or Chinese marinade),
- 4-8 hard or soft boiled large eggs.

Direction
1. Boil your mater stock by placing the master stock inside the instant pot, and close the lid before setting cooking time at 10 minutes. Perform a quick release once the cooking time is completed, and then open the lid gently. Pour the master stock inside a bowl and let it cool.
2. Pressure-cook the eggs by placing a steam basket inside the instant pot, add a cup of running water into the pot before placing the eggs inside the steamer basket. Close the lid and set time at 5 minutes. Open the lid after cooking and place the eggs in an ice bath for about 5 minutes and carefully remove the shells.
3. Infuse the flavor by placing the eggs into a warm bowl of the Chinese master stock, then cover the eggs before placing them in the refrigerator for 2 hours (at least), to allow the eggs soak into the flavor.
4. Serve the eggs either cold or warm inside a sauce pan, after heating for a minute.

Recipe #73: The Instant Pot Chinese Braised Beef Shank

(Total time: 1-hour Servings: 4)

Ingredients

- 1 lb. (454g) of beef shank,
- 1 ½ (375ml) of Chinese master stock.

Direction:

1. Clean the beef by bringing about 1.5 liters of water to boil and then boil the beef shank for 3 minutes inside the instant pot. This will help clean and remove excess fat faster.

2. Pressure-cook the beef by placing the ingredients inside the instant pot and then close the lid and set timer at 35 minutes press natural release after cooking.

3. Let the beef chill then submerge it in the master stock before chilling for 4 hours (or chill overnight).

4. Lice the beef thinly and garnish it with green onion before serving.

Recipe #74: The Cheese Beer-Burger Dip

(Total time: 30 minutes, Servings: 4)

Ingredients

- 1 cup of chopped mushroom,
- 1 finely diced large onion,
- 1 lb. of ground lean beef,
- 1/3 of a cup of beer (preferably, the Sierra Nevada Torpedo IPA),
- 1 teaspoon of salt,
- 1 teaspoon of garlic powder,
- 4 oz. of cream cheese (sliced into 8 pieces),
- 1 tablespoon of flour, and
- 1 cup of shredded sharp cheddar cheese.

Direction

1. Heat 2 teaspoons of olive oil inside the Instant pot and select "sauté". Add the beef, onion and mushrooms. Sauté the beef mix for about 4 minutes until the onion become soften, and beef starts turning dark brown. Drain the excess grease from the beef mix, and stir in the salt, and garlic powder before you pour the beer into the mix. Cover and cook for 10 minutes at high pressure inside the instant pot.

2. Press the Quick release once the cooking time is completed, then add the cream cheese, plus flour across the top of the dip and then stir to combine. Return your instant pot and sauté for about 5 minutes until the dip becomes thickened and cheese is melted.

3. Top up the dip with the shredded cheese and then cover for 5 minutes until the cheese has melted. Serve immediately with corn dips.

Recipe #75: The Mason Jar Steel Cut Oats In Pressure Cooker

(Total time: 25 minutes, servings: 1)

Ingredients
- ½ a cup of steel cut oats,
- 2 tablespoons of pure maple syrup,
- 2 tablespoons of chia seeds,
- ½ a teaspoon of salt,
- ½ cup of extras (nuts, coconut, fresh or dried fruits, and spices),
- 1 cup of water (at room temperature).

Direction
1. Add the oats, chia seeds, syrup, salt, and extras into a pint-size mason jar, then add water (while leaving ½ an inch of head space). Shake the mix until everything is well distributed and the chia seeds are not clumping together.
2. Place a small rack at the bottom of the instant pot and then pour a cup of water into the pot. Choose "high pressure" and set timer at 20 minutes. Turn off the instant pot once cooking is completed, and make use of the natural release. Remove the lid once the valves have dropped.
3. Remove the jars from the pot and place them on cooling rack. Remove the lid of the jar carefully and stir the oats very well before topping it up with a dollop of frozen whipped cream as garnish.

Recipe #76: The Steel Cut Oats

(Total time: 30 minutes, Servings: 2-4)

Ingredients

- 1 cup of steel cut oats,
- 3 cups of water,
- 2 slices of apples or Cinnamon (toppings)

Direction

1. Combine the steel cut oats with water inside the instant pot, then seal the valves and set the timer at 3 minutes at high pressure.

2. Once cooking is completed, let it release its pressure naturally (this will take about 20 minutes). serve the recipe with your preferred toppings

Recipe #77: Instant Pot Lentil Sloppy Joes

(Total time: 40 minutes, Servings: 2-3)

Ingredients

- 2 peeled and diced carrots,
- 1 minced small onion,
- 2 cup of rinsed green lentils,
- 1 cup of water,
- ½ a cup of maple syrup,
- ¼ of a cup of apple cider vinegar,
- 2 teaspoons of salt,
- 2 teaspoons of cumin,
- 2 teaspoons of dry mustard,
- 2 teaspoons of garlic powder, and
- 1 teaspoon each of chili powder and paprika.

Direction

1. Mix all the ingredients inside the instant pot, then stir very well to blend and incorporate the flavor. Cover and set time at 20 minutes before cooking at high pressure. Let the pressure releases naturally after cooking (this should take roughly 10 minutes).

2. Serve the lentil recipe with your homemade rolls, or rice.

Recipe #78: Instant Pot Avocado And Tunas Tapas

(Total time: 20 minutes, serving: 4)

Ingredients:

- 1 can (12 ounces) of packed white tuna – drained,
- 1 dash of balsamic vinegar,
- 1 tablespoon of mayonnaise,
- ½ teaspoon of black pepper (for added taste),
- 3 thinly sliced green onions, for garnishing,
- 1 pinch of salt,
- ½ chopped red bell pepper, and
- 2 ripe halved and pitted avocados.

Direction

1. Get a small to medium size bowl and inside mix the mayonnaise with the tuna, green onions, red pepper and balsamic vinegar.

2. Season the mix with garlic and salt before packing the avocado halves with the Tuna mix.

3. Garnish with the green onions, with a dash of black pepper before you pour them inside the instant pot and sauté at 15 minutes at high pressure. Then press the release manually.

4. Serve immediately.

Recipe #79: Instant Pot Espicanas Con Garbanzos (Spinach With Garbanzos Beans)

(Total time: 25 minutes, Servings: 4)

Ingredients:
- 1 tablespoon of extra virgin olive oil,
- 1 can of drained garbanzo beans,
- 4 cloves of minced garlic,
- ½ a teaspoon of cumin,
- ½ of diced onion,
- ½ teaspoon of salt, and
- 1 box of frozen and chopped spinach (10 ounce of thawed and drained spinach).

Direction

1. Open the Instant pot , and heat the olive oil at high pressure , then cook the garlic and onion inside until they turn translucent(this should take about 5 minutes), with the sauté option.

2. Stir in your spinach, garbanzo beans, salt, and cumin, then use the stirring spoon to mash the beans as the mix start cooking (this should take about 15 minutes)

3. Press the pressure release and transfer into the serving bowl).

Recipe #80: The Instant Pot Sautéed Marinated Shrimp

(Total time: 30 minutes, Servings: 6)
Ingredients:
- 1 cup of olive oil,
- 2 teaspoons of dried oregano,
- ¼ of a cup of fresh parsley (chopped),
- 1 teaspoon of salt,
- 1 juiced lemon,
- 1 teaspoon of ground black pepper,
- 2 tablespoons of hot pepper sauce,
- 2 pounds of large shrimps (peeled and de-veined with the tails still attached),
- 3 cloves of minced garlic,
- Skewers

Direction

1. Get a mixing bowl, and inside, mix the olive oil with the parsley, hot sauce, lemon juice, salt, black pepper, and oregano. Make sure you reserve a small amount for the basting that will be done later. Pour the remainder of the marinade into a big re-sealable plastic bag, alongside the shrimp, then seal and marinate the mix inside the refrigerator for about 2 hours.

2. Turn on the instant pot and set the timer at 20 minutes and choose "sauté". Thread the shrimps onto the pot and piece each near the tail and once close to the head. Dispose the marinade.

3. Cook the shrimps for 10 minutes on each side until they turn opaque. Make sure you are basting frequently with the reserved marinade.

4. Once the cooking is completed, simply press the pressure release manually.

Two-Week Meal Plan For Lectin-Free Body

It is practically impossible to eliminate lectin from raw food but the use of Instant pot to prepare your meals will help destroy lectin and render it ineffective in your body.

A two-week meal plan is designed to help you choose the right low-lectin and possibly lectin-free foods, hence you need to be creative in the way you mix and substitute the food components, to achieve the best possible results.

The veggies you must include in your lectin-free meal plan include; Cruciferous veggies, Broccoli, Cauliflower, Brussel sprouts, arugula, Swiss chard, Watercress, Cabbage, Radicchio, Kale, Celeries, Chives Onions, Artichokes, Beets, Cilantro, Okra, Asparagus, Garlic, Basil and Sea vegetables.

Proteins you should include in your diet include Oily fish, Pastured chicken, and wild-caught fishes, do not consume more than 4 ounces of these at a time.

The oils and good fat you should consume include; Coconut oil, Avocado oil, Sesame seed oil, Walnuts, Extra virgin olive oil, Flaxseed oil, Pecans and Hazelnuts.

For the dressings , seasonings and dressings, you should consider the following; Fresh herbs, vinegar, sea salt, Mustards, fresh spices, and black pepper.

If you are considering snacking, you may want to consider healthy nuts and seeds such as; Macadamia nuts, Half avocado, Pecans, Pistachios, Pine nuts, walnuts, and Brazil nuts.

Week 1 Lectin-Free Meal Plan

	Day	Days	Days				

Meal	1	2	3	Days 4	Days 5	Days 6	Days 7
Breakfast	Artichokes with sautéed navy beans (Instant pot prepared	2 half avocados served with 1 cup of cooked pasta.	chicken and veggie Miso soup	Instant pot sautéed marinated shrimp	steamed-cooked artichoke	The Mediterranean Fried Cabbage served with Bacon and onion	15-minute barbecue chicken soup
Lunch	Fried squid with Pineapple	Instant Pot Mini-Lemon Cheesecakes	The Chinese Broccoli recipe (prepared by instant pot)	Instant pot double bean and Ham soup	Instant pot Korean Ribs	Chicken with Artichoke	Cheese Beer-Burger Dip
Dinner	Espicanas con Garbanzos (Spin	Instant pot taco meat	traditional instant pot Pho-	Instant pot Avocado and	Amish chicken and corn	Instant Pot Aromatic Lamp chops	Creamy Toasted Garlic Mushr

ach with Garbanzos beans)		Ga Soup	Tunas Tapas	soup		ooms	

Week 2 Lectin-Free Meal Plan

Meal	Day 1	Day 2	Day 3	Day 4	Day 5	Day 6	Day 7
Breakfast	Instant pot Rosemary Lemon chicken	Delicious Egg scrambles with spinach	Instant Pot Aromatic Lamp chops	Instant Pot Pineapple Coconut-Lime Rice	Instant pot Chinese Braised Beef Shank	Porridge served with Cinnamon	The Mediterranean Fried Cabbage served with Bacon and onion
Lunch	Instant pot cheese cake	Instant pot taco meat	The traditional instant pot Pho Ga Soup	Cheese Beer-Burger Dip	country chicken stew	Goat Curry in a hurry	Crab meat with Asparagus soup

Dinner	chicken and veggie Miso soup	Sautéed navy beans artichoke	Instant pot Thai Red Curry with Chicken	Instant pot Vietnamese eggplant with spicy sauce	Vegetarian Cassoulet	Instant pot stir fries with beef and green beans	Red snapper Caribbean

You need to take note of the fact that Instant pot method of preparation is needed when preparing these meals- this will guaranty the elimination of lectin from your meals.

Conclusion

It is impossible to find a food that does not contain some amount of lectin, but what is more important is the way you prepare the meals. With an innovative cooking method like Instant pot, it is quite easier to eliminate lectin and render the substance inactive through the application of pressure cooking.

This book has given you an insight into how you can enjoy lectin-free meals that will keep you healthy for many years. It is important that you follow the principles in this book and add your own creativity in preparing the recipes.

Do not allow lectin to ruin your healthy , happy life, make use of the ideal food preparation methods that guaranties a lectin-free lifestyle. Remember, the more lectin you eliminate from your diet, the more you can prevent constant fatigue, and digestive issues.

Part 2

Introduction

Over the years, scientists have worked hard to find the core reason of Chronic Inflammation, and it seems like they may have finally cracked the code.

"Lectins" are now regarded as the culprit for the increase of inflammatory diseases. Initially thought to be harmless, this protein is present in a variety of foods that we previously considered "Healthy" and is slowly breaks down our body from the inside!

Afraid? Well, don't be! The Lectin Free Diet (Plant Paradox) is here to save the day.

Since the sections and recipes in this book are dedicated to novices, the first few chapters fully explain the fundamental concepts of Lectins diet while walking you through the basics of healthy eating as well. Once you learned the basics, the amazing healthy and delicious Lectin Free recipes will inspire you to explore the Plant Paradox Lectin Free Diet further and stay healthy for the long run!

Is that enough for you? Off course not!

All recipes in this book are made just by one pot! They may be made by an Instant Pot or a Slow Cooker, which will save you too much time and money but still have your favorite and nutritional lectin free dishes!

Cherish this book! Not only will it be your complete guide of Lectin Free Diet, but also will be your life-changing companion for your every meal! Too be healthy, happy, and stress-free by this amazing cookbook!

Welcome to the One Pot Lectin Free world!

Chapter 1: Essentials Of The Lectin Free Diet

What are Exactly Lectins?

In the simplest terms, Lectins are the proteins that are responsible for binding cell membranes together.

They have a sugar binding nature and are the "Glyco" section of Glycoconjugates present in the cell membranes.

They assist other cells to interact with each other and unite without the aid of the immune mechanism. Lectins are a key factor when considering inter-cell bindings.

Why Are Lectins Bad for Our Health?

While Lectin is found in most parts of all plants, the "Seeds" are consumed the most by people and are considered one of the original ways through which humans are exposed to Lectins.

According to recent studies, it was found that Lectins are incredibly toxic to the human body.

These harmful proteins cause widespread inflammation all around the body, which leads to various side effects including, but not limited to unwanted weight gain, fogginess, digestion issues, and so on.

All these side effects give Lectins the notorious title of being "Anti-Nutrients" as they not only cause inflammation but also restrict the absorption of essential nutrients required by the body.

A Deeper Looking at the Science Behind Lectins in Detail

Lectins are generally carbohydrate-binding proteins that tend to attach to cell membranes.

They act as "Communicators" between other cells and allow them to interact with the environment and bind with each other.

It should be noted that there are different types of Lectins found in living organisms. The Lectins in plants are primarily located in their roots and seed with the lowest amount available in the leaves.

While there are thousands of different types of Lectins present, researchers took their time to break them down into thirteen significant classifications with only two classes (namely agglutinins and prolamins) causing the most damage.

These two cause a significant impact on how the gut and immune system of the body functions, causing a severe inflammatory response.

When your intestinal wall is permeated by these Lectins, proteins tend to seep out into the bloodstream.

At that time, the Lectin binds to Glycoproteins that are found on the surface of most cells and antibodies, turning them into abnormal entities.

These anomalous cells travel to assorted parts of your body, which ultimately causes the body's natural reaction to trigger the autoimmune response that leads to severe inflammation.

Understanding the Core Concepts of Lectin-Free Diet In a Short Time

A former heart surgeon called Dr. Steven Gundry established this particular form of diet.

To summarize in brief, the Lectin Free diet is a form of elimination diet precisely designed to remove any ingredients from everyday food that is considered packed with a high amount of Lectins.

Incidentally, due to our hectic schedule, we often eat seemingly "Healthy" foods packed with Lectins! We fail to understand the severe implications, and they cause significant harm to the body after a prolonged period.

This is where we can briefly discuss inflammations.

What Exactly are Glutens?

Before the discovery of Lectins, Glutens were one of the most controversial entities that forced people into debates of whether it was good or bad.

There is a powerful connection between Glutens and Lectins. Yet, before establishing and explaining that, it is essential to have an understanding of what "Glutens" actually are.

Strictly speaking, Glutens are a family of protein found in grains such as barley, wheat, rye, and spelt.

The most common Gluten containing grain that we consume is Wheat.

When flour is mixed with water, Gluten is responsible for the texture. This glue-like property helps elasticize the dough and allows bread to rise when baked.

Nonetheless, there is a large portion of the population unable to tolerate gluten.

While most people can digest it, others suffer from various diseases such as wheat allergy, inflammation, irritable bowel syndrome, celiac diseases and so on.

The Role of Gluten in the Diet and how it Affects Our Health

Some individuals believe that cutting down "Gluten" from their diet will naturally help them to stay healthy and fit.

The reason is the fact that Gluten is thought to be a type of Lectin, primarily belonging to the "Prolamin" class.

There are many types of Lectins, and cutting down Glutens from your diet will only save you from one of two harmful classes of Lectin.

You may still get Lectins from other foods, if you are not careful!

What is an Inflammation?

This brings us to our next issue with Lectins and Glutens, Inflammation.

Amongst the many side effects of Lectins exposure, Inflammation is at the top of the list. But what does inflammation mean?

Let us elaborate.

Inflammation is a vital aspect of our body's immune system and is an attempt to heal itself from any anomaly/defend itself from foreign organisms such as bacteria, virus and of course, repair damaged tissues.

Without natural inflammation, the wounds in our body would never heal and infections would eventually become deadly!

So far, so good, right?

This very effect can also cause extreme discomfort if "False" signals are sent to the body to initiate an unwanted inflammatory impact.

Due to the nature of an inflammation, they are divided into two categories, acute and chronic.

Acute inflammation arises when you get a bruise, cut, sprained ankle, etc. These are the natural response of the body to heal you.

On the other hand, Chronic Inflammations are the "Dire" kind; not useful to the body. Instead, they tend to occur due to certain diseases such as osteoarthritis and various auto-immune diseases such as lupus, allergies, inflammatory bowel disease, rheumatoid arthritis, and so on.

Relationship between Lectins and Inflammation You Must Know

It has already been established what Lectins and how damaging they are to the human body, we learned what inflammation is.

Now, let us discover what is the correlation between them.

Lectins are thought to cause inflammation in the body that can occur in your bloodstream or outside the digestive tract (due to the leakage of Lectins).

When this happens, our body starts to experience a wide range of symptoms depending on what we have eaten.

These range from bloating to severe vomiting or diarrhea.

Initially, they remain at a tolerable level, however, if you keep exposing your body to more Lectins (result in a greater rate of inflammation), it is possible these symptoms become something severe and significantly damage the body.

Just as a revelation, studies have shown that almost 20% of Rheumatoid arthritis is caused by consuming Lectin containing vegetables or ingredients.

The Important Ins and Outs of a Lectin Free Diet

That being said, be inquisitive as to what you eat and what to avoid, right?

According to the creator of the diet, Dr. Gundry, the following foods will ease you into the diet:

- Olives and Olive Oil: Olives are generally low in Lectin and are safe to consume on a Lectin free diet
- Avocados: Though it is a fruit, you can enjoy Avocados in Lectin free recipes
- Mushrooms: You can choose from a wide variety of mushrooms available in the market.
- Celery
- Asparagus
- Cruciferous Vegetables: veggies such as Brussels sprouts, broccoli, or cauliflower are veggies that provide you with great nutrients while being low in Lectins
- Sweet Potatoes: even if potatoes are considered to be high in Lectins, sweet potatoes are amazing for a Lectin Free diet. Enjoy the health benefits of potatoes while keeping your Lectins in check
- Pasture-raised meat: When considering meat, try to go for pasture-raised meat as they will help you meet up your daily protein need.

And on the opposite side, here are items to avoid as much as possible to keep your Lectins down:

- Corn: This plant should be avoided as they are high on Lectins.
- Grains: Any grain should be avoided during this diet. If you need grains in your diet, go for things that are made from White Flour instead of Wheat Flour as wheat flour contains more Lectins.
- Fruits: When considering fruit, always go for seasonal fruits
- Legumes such as beans, lentils, peas, and peanuts are to be avoided
- Squash
- Casein A2 Milk: Always make sure to avoid Casein A2 Milk

- All nightshade vegetables such as eggplant, peppers, potatoes tomatoes, etc. Keep in mind that tomatoes and peppers can be used in moderate amount if you properly deseed them and peel them (in case of tomato). This helps lower the Lectin levels.

How Lectins Negatively Affect our Health

Uncontrolled inflammation, which may result from excessive Lectin input leads to a variety of harmful side effects.
Some of them include:

- **Type 1 Diabetes:** Type 1 Diabetes will cause the immune system to attack and destroy insulin-producing cells in your pancreas that ultimately disrupts the regulation of sugar levels in your body.
- **Rheumatoid Arthritis:** RA causes the immune system to attack specific joints that results in considerable discomfort and pain.
- **Psoriatic Arthritis:** This causes the skin cells to multiply rapidly, resulting in red and scaly patches (called plaques) on the skin.
- **Multiple Sclerosis:** MS tends to damage the protective coating that surrounds nerve cells (known as myelin sheath) and affects the transmission of neural messages between the brain and body. This often leads to weakness, balance issues, etc.
- **Inflammatory Bowel Syndromes:** This disease will irritate the intestinal lining.
- **Graves' disease:** This disease attacks the thyroid gland in your neck and causes it to produce too much hormone, resulting in a severe imbalance.
- **Cancer:** Cancerous tumors tend to secrete substances that attract cytokines and free-radicals that further cause inflammation and helps the tumors to survive. If you suffer

from Inflammation, it will make the condition of the Cancer much worse.
- **Alzheimer's:** The brain does not contain pain receptors, but that doesn't mean that it cannot feel the effects of inflammation. Researchers have recently discovered that people with a high level of Omega-6 fatty acids have a bigger chance of suffering from Alzheimer's disease, which hampers your memory and makes you forget things.

Easy but Effective Lectin Free Substitutes for the Pantry

Initially, you may start to feel that most of your favorite meals are packed with Lectins and you will not enjoy good foods anymore.

That is not the case; there are great substitutes that allow you to take pleasure in your meals while staying Lectin free!

With the right ingredients, with ease you can adapt to your new cooking and healthier lifestyle.

Some of the usual substitutes are as follows:
- Replace wheat flour with almond flour
- Replace soy sauce with coconut aminos
- Replace regular mayonnaise with Duke's Mayonnaise
- Replace regular butter with ghee (clarified butter)
- Replace regular BBQ sauce with "NO Ketchup BBQ Sauce."
- Replace milk with almond milk or coconut milk
- Replace sugar with stevia
- Replace arrowroot powder instead of cornstarch

These tips should help you convert most of your standard recipes to Lectin Friendly ones.

Main Advantages of a Lectin Free (Plant Paradox) Diet

While there are many benefits to reap from a Lectin Free diet, some of the more crucial ones are:
- Decrease the chances of suffering from chronic inflammation
- Improve your heart condition
- Defends you from cancer
- Helps you fend off depression
- Help you tackle various autoimmune diseases such as rheumatoid arthritis, diabetes and celiac diseases

And a lot of more!

Fantastic Tips for Your Lectin Free Journey To Be Known

Aside from following the strict diet and cutting down all sorts of Lectin ingredients, undoubtedly other steps can expand the number of Lectins and depend on how you prepare your foods.

- **Pressure Cooking:** Pressure cooking has been considered one of the healthiest ways of preparing food as most of the nutrients are preserved correctly. The pressure cooker also does a great job of destroying the Lectins present in plants. If you are using ingredients such as beans, tomatoes, quinoa or even potatoes, pressure cooking them will destroy the Lectins and make them consumable.
- **Choosing the Right Color:** Healthy food habits contribute to lowering Lectins as well. Nevertheless, there is a catch. People often recommend the "BROWN" of anything when considering healthy food; brown rice, brown flour, and so on. In case of Lectins, it is advised you do the opposite. The best step is to avoid grains altogether, but if you happen to like grains, use White Rice instead of brown and white bread instead of brown bread.
- **Peeling and Deseeding: The** majority of vegetables have the highest concentration of Lectins in their skin and seeds. Thus, it is recommended to thoroughly peel and deseed

fruits and vegetables to reduce the amount of Lectins present.

Asides from those, you may also opt for:
- Boiling
- Sprouting
- Fermenting

To lower the Lectin count.

Chapter 2: Easing Into The Lectin Free Diet

With all that said, you must be wondering how to start following the diet, right?

The best way to do this is to start on a trial period and assess the results.

Start with a trial period

To begin, perhaps a good step would be a trial period of one week. During that week, you will strictly adhere to the Lectin Free diet and make all the necessary changes as required by the Lectin Free Diet.

Keep in mind that during the first few days of your diet, you may experience some uneven symptoms. Don't worry as these are temporary and go away once your body adjusts to the new diet.

If you feel that taking all the Lectin Free food would be difficult, an alternative way is to remove one Lectin Food from your regular diet each week.

This gives you the chance to measure the changes and helps you understand which Lectin foods are the most sensitive, and gives you a broader idea of your Lectin intolerance.

If you are in a hurry, you can also opt for taking various Antibody tests that show certain types of Lectins, but these tests are not exhaustive and have the chance to give an unclear report.

Therefore, physicians and dieticians always recommended to manually assessing the impacts of removing Lectin food one by one.

The next step is to evaluate how you feel and what you should do. You can do three things from here.

What to do if you feel better

If you think that cutting down your Lectin has improved your health, then the most appropriate thing to do is to consider extending the period of your test and think about following the diet in the long term.

The path forward will depend on how you followed the diet during your Test Period.

If you cut all Lectin Free food at once, continue that routine.

If you cut the Lectin packed food one by one, keep following that!

The goal is to move forward with the method that you are most comfortable with.

B sure to follow the advice provided at the end of the chapter to decrease your Lectin count further.

Two important things to note:

- During this period, track the Lectin free foods that make you feel better. Incorporate those ingredients into more recipes and create your diet regime surrounding those recipes.
- Try to gauge how much better you feel reducing the Lectins in your diet. Track simple points such as any energy changes, sleep patterns, physical condition, etc. These will not only keep you motivated but will also help you appraise your progress.

What to do if nothing has changed?

Once your trial period is over, if there are no noticeable differences in your health, go back and review what you may have done wrong.

Naturally, don't cut down all Lectin Food in one go (unless you are comfortable with it). The reason why you did not experience a difference might result from not removing enough Lectin from your diet.

In that case, do another trial week and limit more Lectin packed food compared to your previous week.

What to do if situations have gotten worse?

The worst-case scenario is after the trial week, you might feel worse than you felt before.

This may happen for many different reasons, especially if you have underlying health issues.

In this scenario, consult your doctor as soon as possible and perform antibody test accordingly.

It will indicate if you have a specific intolerance to a Lectin classification.

Chapter 3: Easy-To-Follow Breakfast Recipes

Mesmerizing Cauliflower Pudding

(Prepping time: 10 minutes\ Cooking time: 10 minutes |For 4 servings)

Ingredients

- 1 and ½ cups unsweetened coconut milk
- 1 cup water
- 1 cup cauliflower rice (florets pulsed in food processor)
- 2 teaspoon organic ground cinnamon powder
- 1 teaspoon pure vanilla extract
- Pinch of salt

Directions

1. Add the listed ingredients to your Instant Pot and stir
2. Lock lid and cook on HIGH pressure for 20 minutes
3. Release pressure naturally over 10 minutes
4. Serve and enjoy!

Nutrition Values (Per Serving)

- Calories: 213
- Fat: 21g
- Carbohydrates: 7g
- **Protein: 2g**

Cool Prosciutto Cane

(Prepping time: 2 minutes\ Cooking time: 5 minutes |For 4 servings)

Ingredients

- 1 pound thick asparagus
- 80 ounces prosciutto, sliced

Directions

1. Add the listed ingredients to your Instant Pot and stir
2. Lock lid and cook on HIGH pressure for 20 minutes
3. Release pressure naturally over 10 minutes
4. Serve and enjoy!

Nutrition Values (Per Serving)

- Calories: 212
- Fat: 14g
- Carbohydrates: 11g
- Protein: 12g

Simple And Straightforward Broccoli

(Prepping time: 3 minutes\ Cooking time: 4 minutes |For 2 servings)

Ingredients

- 1 medium broccoli
- Salt and pepper as needed
- ¾ cup water

Directions

1. Add ¾ cup of water to the pot
2. Chop up the broccoli into florets and place them on a steamer rack
3. Place the rack on top of your pot
4. Lock up the lid and cook on HIGH pressure for 2 minutes
5. Once done ,allow the pressure naturally
6. Serve with a seasoning of salt and pepper

Nutrition Values (Per Serving)

- Calories: 33
- Fat: 3g
- Carbohydrates: 2g
- Protein: 1g

Easy Going Mushroom Bowl

(Prepping time: 10 minutes\ Cooking time: 20 minutes |For 4 servings)

Ingredients

- 8 cups beef stock
- 1 pound baby bella mushrooms, sliced
- 1 medium onion, diced
- 2 celery stalks, diced
- 2 carrots, diced
- 4 garlic cloves, chopped
- 4 sprigs thyme
- 1 sprig sage
- 1 teaspoon salt
- ¼ teaspoon fresh ground pepper
- ¼ teaspoon garlic powder

Directions

1. Add the listed ingredients to your Instant Pot
2. Stir and lock lid
3. Cook on HIGH pressure for 20 minutes
4. Release pressure naturally over 10 minutes
5. Serve and enjoy!

Nutrition Values (Per Serving)

- Calories : 114
- Fat : 1g
- Carbohydrates : 15g
- Protein : 7g

Appetizing Chicken Balls

(Prepping time: 10 minutes\ Cooking time: 20 minutes |For 24 servings)

Ingredients

- 1 and ½ pound ground chicken
- ¾ cup almond meal
- 1 teaspoon sea salt
- 2 garlic cloves, minced
- 2 green onions, thinly sliced
- 2 tablespoon ghee
- 6 tablespoons hot sauce
- 4 tablespoons extra ghee for frying
- ½ a onion, chopped

Directions

1. Take a large bowl and add chicken, almond meal, salt, minced cloves, green onions
2. Combine everything well and form 1-2 inch wide balls using the mixture
3. Set your pot Saute mode and ghee, place the balls and brown them for a few minutes
4. Do in batches until all balls are done
5. Take a bowl and add hot sauce and ghee, microwave to make a sauce
6. Add browned balls to your Instant Pot alongside sauce
7. Lock lid and cook on POULTRY mode for 20 minutes
8. Release pressure naturally over 10 minutes
9. Serve and enjoy!

Nutrition Values (Per Serving)

- Calories: 206
- Fat: 13g
- Carbohydrates: 8g
- **Protein: 15g**

Very Nutty Faux "Oatmeal"

(Prepping time: 10 minutes\ Cooking time: 8 hours |For 6 servings)

Ingredients
- 1 tablespoon coconut oil
- 1 cup coconut milk
- 1 cup unsweetened shredded coconut
- ½ cup pecans, chopped
- ½ cup almonds, sliced
- 2 tablespoon stevia
- 1 avocado, diced
- 1 teaspoon ground cinnamon
- ¼ teaspoon ground nutmeg
- ½ cup blueberries, garnish

Directions
1. Grease the inner pot of your Slow Cooker with coconut oil
2. Place coconut milk, coconut, pecans, almonds, avocado, stevia, cinnamon and nutmeg to your Slow Cooker
3. Cover and cook on LOW for 8 hours
4. Stir the mix until you have your desired texture
5. Serve topped with blueberries
6. Enjoy!

Nutrition Values (per serving)
- Calories: 365
- Fat: 33g
- Carbohydrates: 10g
- **Protein: 14g**

Early Morning Good Sausage Meatloaf

(Prepping time: 10 minutes\ Cooking time: 3 hours |For 6 servings)

Ingredients

- 1 tablespoon extra-virgin olive oil
- 2 pounds ground pork
- 1 sweet onion, chopped
- ½ cup almond flour
- 2 teaspoon garlic, minced
- 2 teaspoon dried oregano
- 1 teaspoon dried thyme
- 1 teaspoon fennel seeds
- 1 teaspoon freshly ground black pepper
- ½ teaspoon salt
- 1 cup mashed banana or applesauce

Directions

1. Grease the insert of your Slow Cooker with olive oil
2. Take a large bowl and add pork, onion, banana/applesauce, almond flour, oregano, garlic, thyme, fennel seeds, pepper and salt
3. Mix well and pour the meat mix into the Slow Cooker
4. Shape it into loaf, leaving about ½ inch between the sides of the meat and inner pot wall
5. Cover and cook for 3 hours on LOW until the internal temperature reaches 150 degree Fahrenheit
6. Slice and serve. Enjoy!

Nutrition Values (per serving)

- Calories: 341
- Fat: 27g
- Carbohydrates: 1g
- Protein: 21g

Creamy Nice Broccoli Casserole

(Prepping time: 15 minutes\ Cooking time: 6 hours |For 6 servings)

Ingredients

- 1 tablespoon extra-virgin olive oil
- 1 pound broccoli, cut into florets
- 1 pound cauliflower, cut into florets
- ¼ cup almond flour
- 2 cups coconut milk
- ½ teaspoon ground nutmeg
- Pinch of fresh ground black pepper
- 1 and ½ cups cashew cream

Directions

1. Grease the Slow Cooker inner pot with olive oil
2. Place broccoli and cauliflower to your Slow Cooker
3. Take a small bowl and stir in almond flour, coconut milk, pepper, 1 cup of cashew cream
4. Pour coconut milk mixture over vegetables and top casserole with remaining cashew cream
5. Cover and cook on LOW for 6 hours
6. Server and enjoy!

Nutrition Values (per serving)

- Calories: 377
- Fat: 32g
- Carbohydrates: 12g
- **Protein: 16g**

Bacon And Kale

(Prepping time: 15 minutes\ Cooking time: 6 hours |For 4 servings)

Ingredients

- 2 tablespoons bacon fat
- 2 pounds kale, rinsed and chopped
- 2 bacon slices, cooked and chopped
- 2 teaspoons garlic, minced
- 2 cups vegetable broth
- Salt as needed
- Fresh ground black pepper

Directions

1. Grease the inner pot with bacon fat
2. Add kale, garlic, bacon, broth to insert and toss
3. Cover and cook on LOW for 6 hours
4. Season with salt and pepper
5. Serve and enjoy!

Nutrition Values (per serving)

- Calories: 147
- Fat: 10g
- Carbohydrates: 7g
- **Protein: 7g**

Chapter 4: Mouth-Watering Fish And Seafood Recipes

Shrimp And Sausage Bowl

(Prepping time: 10 minutes\ Cooking time: 4 minutes |For 4 servings)

Ingredients
- 1 and ½ pounds sweet potatoes, peeled and cubed
- 1 and ½ pounds shrimp, peeled and deveined
- 3 smoked sausages, sliced
- 1 tablespoon low-sodium coconut aminos
- 1 tablespoon organic Cajun seasoning
- ½ cup ghee, melted
- ½ teaspoon garlic powder
- Pinch of salt and pepper
- 3 cups low sodium vegetable broth

Directions
1. Add potato cubes, sausage to your Pot
2. Add broth and coconut aminos
3. Stir well and lock the lid
4. Cook on HIGH pressure for 4 minutes
5. Quick release the pressure
6. Add shrimp, ghee, garlic powder, salt, black pepper and Cajun seasoning
7. Stir well
8. Press Saute mode and let it cook until shrimp is no longer pink
9. Ladle into bowls and garnish with parsley
10. Enjoy!

Nutrition Values (Per Serving)
- Calories: 663
- Fat: 38g
- Carbohydrates: 33g
- **Protein: 43g**

Tasty Sweet Chili Tilapia Dish

(Prepping time: 10 minutes\ Cooking time: 10 minutes |For 4 servings)

Ingredients

- 4 boneless, skinless Tilapia fish fillets
- 2 teaspoons olive oil
- ¼ cup coconut aminos
- Pinch of salt and pepper
- 2 teaspoons crushed red pepper flakes
- Handful of fresh baby spinach, chopped
- 1 teaspoon low-sodium coconut aminos
- ¼ cup homemade Lectin-Free Chili Sauce

Directions

1. Take a bowl and add coconut aminos, black pepper, red pepper flakes, salt and baby spinach
2. Mix well
3. Coat the tilapia fillets with the marinade
4. Take another bowl and add chili sauce, coconut aminos and stir
5. Set your pot to Saute mode and add olive oil, let it heat up
6. Add fillets and Saute for 2-3 minutes per side
7. Transfer fillets to serving platter
8. Top with chili sauce and serve
9. Enjoy!

Nutrition Values (Per Serving)

- Calories: 118
- Fat: 4g
- Carbohydrates: 1g
- **Protein: 21g**

Salmon And Broccoli Medley

(Prepping time: 10 minutes\ Cooking time: 4 minutes |For 4 servings)

Ingredients

- 2 and ½ ounces salmon fillets
- 2 and ½ ounces broccoli, chopped in florets
- 9 ounces new potatoes
- 1 teaspoon almond butter
- Pepper as needed
- Crushed sunflower seeds
- Fresh herbs

Directions

1. Add ½ cup water to your Instant Pot
2. Season potatoes with sunflower seeds, fresh herb and pepper
3. Season salmon with broccoli florets and sunflower seeds and pepper
4. Add potatoes to steaming rack and smother with butter
5. Transfer to your pot
6. Lock lid and cook on STEAM for 2 minutes
7. Quick release
8. Add broccoli florets and salmon, close lid and STEAM cook for 2 minutes more
9. Quick release
10. Serve and enjoy!

Nutrition Values (Per Serving)

- Calories: 701
- Fat: 39g
- Carbohydrates: 30g
- Protein: 57g

Sharp Garlic And Butter Swordfish

(Prepping time: 10 minutes\ Cooking time: 25 minutes |For 4 servings)

Ingredients

- 5 sword fish fillets
- ½ cup melted almond butter
- 6 garlic cloves, chopped
- 1 tablespoon black pepper

Directions

1. Take a mixing bowl and toss in all of your garlic, black pepper alongside the melted butter
2. Take a parchment paper and place your fish fillet in that paper
3. Cover it up with the butter mixture and wrap up the fish
4. Repeat the process until all of your fish are wrapped up
5. Let it cook for 2 and a half hours and release the pressure naturally
6. Serve

Nutrition Values (Per Serving)

- Calories: 379
- Fat: 26g
- Carbohydrates: 1g
- Protein: 34g

Authentic Ginger Tilapia

(Prepping time: 10 minutes\ Cooking time: 5 minutes |For 4 servings)

Ingredients

- 1 pound Tilapia fish fillets
- 3 tablespoons low-sodium coconut aminos
- 2 tablespoons white vinegar
- 2 fresh garlic cloves, minced
- Pinch of salt and pepper
- 1 tablespoon olive oil
- 2 tablespoons fresh ginger, julienned
- ¼ cup fresh scallions, julienned
- ¼ cup fresh cilantro, chopped

Directions

1. Take a bowl and add coconut aminos, white vinegar, minced garlic, salt, white pepper and mix well
2. Add tilapia fish and carefully spoon the sauce over and coat it
3. Marinate for 2 hours
4. Add 2 cups of water to the Instant Pot
5. Add steamer rack to the Instant Pot and remove fillets from marinade, transfer them to Steamer Rack
6. Lock lid and cook on LOW pressure for 2 minutes
7. Quick release pressure
8. Transfer fillets to serving dish and discard water
9. Set your pot to Saute mode and add olive oil, let it heat up
10. Add julienned ginger and Saute for a few seconds
11. Add scallions, cilantro and Saute for 2 minutes
12. Stir in remaining marinade and let it heat up
13. Spoon the sauce over fish
14. Enjoy!

Nutrition Values (Per Serving)

- Calories: 176
- Fat: 6g
- Carbohydrates: 4.9g
- **Protein: 25g**

Coconut Shrimp

(Prepping time: 5 minutes\ Cooking time: 2 hours |For 4 servings)

Ingredients

- 1 pound shrimp, with shells
- 3 and ¾ cups light coconut milk
- 1 and ¾ cups water
- ½ cup Thai Red curry sauce
- 2 and ½ teaspoons lemon garlic seasoning
- ¼ cup cilantro

Directions

1. Add coconut milk, red curry sauce, water, lemon garlic seasoning and cilantro to your Slow Cooker
2. Give it a nice stir
3. Cook on HIGH for 2 hours
4. **Add shrimp and cook for another 15-30 minutes**
5. Garnish with some cilantro and serve!

Nutrition Values (per serving)

- Calories: 576
- Fat: 22g
- Carbohydrates: 63g
- **Protein: 32g**

Asparagus Tilapia Dish

(Prepping time: 20 minutes\ Cooking time:2 hours |For 4 servings)

Ingredients

- A bunch of asparagus
- 4-6 Tilapia fillets
- 8-12 tablespoons lemon juice
- Pepper for seasoning
- Lemon juice for seasoning
- ½ tablespoon of clarified butter for each fillet

Directions

1. Cut single pieces of foil for the fillets
2. Divide the bundle of asparagus into even number depending on the number of your fillets
3. Lay the fillets on each of the piece of foil and sprinkle pepper and add a teaspoon of lemon juice
4. **Add clarified butter and top with asparagus**
5. Fold the foil over the fish and seal the ends
6. Repeat with all the fillets and transfer to cooker
7. Cook on HIGH for 2 hours
8. Enjoy!

Nutrition Values (per serving)

- Calories: 576
- Calories: 381
- Fat: 25g
- Carbohydrates: 4g
- Protein: 35g

Amazing Salmon Curry

(Prepping time: 10 minutes\ Cooking time: 2 hours 45 minutes |For 4 servings)

Ingredients

- 6 piece salmon fillets, skinless
- 1 large onion, chopped
- 6 garlic cloves, chopped
- 2 teaspoons ginger, grated
- 3 stalks celery, chopped
- 2 carrots, chopped
- 2 cans coconut milk
- ½ cup vegetable stock
- 1 and ½ teaspoon coriander
- 1 and ½ teaspoons cumin
- 1 teaspoon chili powder
- 1 cup red bell pepper paste
- 2 teaspoon smoked paprika
- 1 teaspoon turmeric
- ½ teaspoon pepper
- ½ teaspoon salt
- Cilantro, parsley, chili flakes, all chopped for garnish

Directions

1. Add 2 cans of coconut milk to the slow cooker
2. Add red bell pepper paste
3. Add vegetable stock, coriander, cumin, paprika, turmeric
4. **Season with salt and pepper**
5. Stir in the remaining ingredients
6. Place salmon pieces into the slow cooker and add onion, garlic, carrots, celery and ginger
7. Place lid and cook on LOW for 2 hours and 4 minutes
8. Garnish and serve!

Nutrition Values (per serving)

- Calories : 362
- Fat : 26g
- Carbohydrates : g
- Protein : 24g

Crazy Slow Salmon Fillet

(Prepping time: 5 minutes\ Cooking time: 1 hour | For 4 servings)

Ingredients

- 2 tablespoon ghee
- 1 small onion, sliced
- 1 cup water
- ½ cup vegetable
- 4 salmon fillets
- 1 sprig fresh dill
- Sea salt as needed
- Black pepper as needed
- 1 quartered lemon, for garnish

Directions

1. Grease the slow cooker with ghee
2. Add onion slices to your pot and pour water
3. Add chicken broth
4. **Cook on HIGH for 30 minutes (lid open)**
5. Place fillets on top of the cooked onion and add lemon juice alongside fresh dill
6. Cover lid and cook on HIGH for 30 minutes more
7. Season with pepper and salt
8. Garnish with lemon and enjoy!

Nutrition Values (per serving)

- Calories: 576
- Calories: 381
- Fat: 25g
- Carbohydrates: 4g
- Protein: 35g

Chapter 5: Graceful Lectin Free Meat Recipes

Pork And Cabbage Platter

(Prepping time: 10 minutes\ Cooking time: 5 minutes |For 4 servings)

Ingredients

- 1 and ½ pounds ground pork
- 2 tablespoons olive oil
- 2 shallots, peeled and finely chopped
- 1 cup low-sodium chicken broth
- 2 cups cauliflower florets, chopped
- 6 cups fresh green cabbage, shredded
- 2 garlic cloves, minced
- Pinch of each salt and pepper

Directions

1. Set your pot to Saute mode and add olive oil
2. Add ground pork, chopped shallots, minced garlic and cook until browned
3. Add cauliflower, salt, cabbage and pepper to your Instant Pot
4. Close lid and cook on HIGH pressure for 3 minutes
5. Quick release the pressure
6. Transfer to platter and enjoy!

Nutrition Values (Per Serving)

- Calories: 163
- Fat: 4g
- Carbohydrates: 9g
- **Protein: 21g**

Big Time Buffalo Wings And Cauliflower *

(Prepping time: 1 minutes\ Cooking time: 5 minutes |For 4 servings)

Ingredients

- ½ cup Frank's Hot Sauce
- ¼ cup ghee
- 2 pounds chicken wings
- ½ head cauliflower, cut into florets

Directions

1. Add a cup of water to you pot
2. Place a trivet
3. Arrange chicken wings on top of trivet and arrange cauliflower on top chicken wings
4. Lock lid and cook on HIGH pressure for 5 minutes
5. Release naturally over 5-10 minutes
6. Toss the wings and cauliflower in buffalo sauce
7. Serve and enjoy!

Nutrition Values (Per Serving)

- Calories: 179
- Fat: 1.2g
- Carbohydrates: 31g
- **Protein: 12g**

Harissa Beef

(Prepping time: 10 minutes\ Cooking time: 15 minutes |For 4 servings)

Ingredients

- 4 pounds beef roast, trimmed

- 4 garlic cloves, minced
- 1 teaspoon ground cumin
- 1 teaspoon ground coriander
- ½ teaspoon chili powder
- 2 tablespoons Harissa paste
- 1 cup beef stock

Directions

1. Add garlic, cumin, salt, chili powder, coriander, harissa paste to a bowl and mix well
2. Spread the mix over the beef and rub generously
3. Transfer meat to Instant Pot
4. Add stock
5. Lock lid and cook on HIGH pressure for 25 minutes
6. Release the pressure naturally over 10 minutes
7. Serve and enjoy!

Nutrition Values (Per Serving)

- Calories:427
- Fat: 14g
- Carbohydrates: 0.7g
- Protein: 69g

Thick Artichoke Pork Chops

(Prepping time: 10 minutes\ Cooking time: 24 minutes |For 4 servings)

Ingredients

- 2 tablespoons ghee
- 2 piece bone-in-pork loin, 2 inch each
- 3 ounces pancetta, diced
- 2 teaspoons ground black pepper
- 1 medium shallot, minced
- 4 pieces (2 inch long) lemon zest strips
- 1 teaspoon dried rosemary
- 2 teaspoons garlic, minced
- 9 ounce artichoke heart quarters
- ¼ cup chicken broth

Directions

1. Set your pot to Saute mode and add pancetta, cook for 5 minutes
2. Transfer the browned pancetta to a plate and season your chops with pepper
3. Add the chops to your pot and cook for 4 minutes
4. Transfer the chops to a plate and keep repeating until they all of them are browned
5. Add shallots to the pot and cook for 1 minute
6. Add lemon zest, garlic, ,rosemary and garlic and stir until aromatic
7. After a while, stir in broth and artichokes
8. Return the pancetta back to the cooker
9. return the chops to your pot
10. Lock up the lid and let it cook for about 24 minutes at high pressure
11. Release pressure quickly
12. Unlock and transfer the chops to a carving board

13. Slice up the eye of your meat off the bone and slice the meat into strips
14. Divide in serving bowls and sauce ladled up

Nutrition Values (Per Serving)
- Calories: 245
- Fat: 45g
- Carbohydrates: 12g
- **Protein: 48g**

The Swedish Pork Roast

(Prepping time: 10 minutes\ Cooking time: 85 minutes |For 4 servings)

Ingredients

- 4 pounds boneless pork loin roast
- 1 tablespoon olive oil
- 2 cups low-sodium beef broth
- 1 large yellow onion, peeled and grated
- 8 garlic cloves, crushed
- 3 tablespoon swerve
- 2 tablespoon salt
- 1 tablespoon fresh parsley, chopped
- 1 teaspoon organic ground cumin powder
- ½ teaspoon organic ground cardamom powder
- 1 teaspoon fresh ground nutmeg
- 1 teaspoon black pepper

Directions

1. Season pork loin roast with swerve, salt, cardamom powder, cumin powder, pepper
2. Set your pot to Saute mode and add olive oil
3. Add garlic, onion and cook for 4 minutes
4. Add pork roast and sear all sides
5. Stir in beef broth and lock lid
6. Cook on HIGH pressure for 85 minutes
7. Naturally release the pressure over 10 minutes
8. Transfer roast to serving platter and let it rest for 10 minutes
9. Slice and pour cooking liquid over the slices
10. Serve and enjoy!

Nutrition Values (Per Serving)

- Calories: 287
- Fat: 7g
- Carbohydrates: 6g
- **Protein: 48g**

Succulent Pot Roast

(Prepping time: 10 minutes\ Cooking time: 8 hours |For 6 servings)

Ingredients

- 2 pounds beef chuck roast, trimmed
- 1 pound russet potatoes, peeled and quartered
- 1 pound baby carrots
- 1 medium yellow onion, quartered
- 1 tablespoon steak seasoning
- ½ cup beef broth
- Salt
- Freshly ground black pepper

Directions

1. Cut roast into 4 equal pieces
2. Arrange beef, carrot, potatoes, onion in your Slow Cooker
3. Sprinkle beef and veggies with steak seasoning
4. Pour broth
5. Cover and cook on LOW for 8 hours
6. Transfer beef to cutting board and slice, transfer to serving dish
7. Serve with veggies and juice from slow cooker
8. Season with salt and pepper and enjoy!

Nutrition Values (per serving)

- Calories: 313
- Fat: 11g
- Carbohydrates: 19g
- **Protein: 33g**

Cilantro And Lime (Shredded) Pork

(Prepping time: 5 minutes\ Cooking time: 8 hours |For 6 servings)

Ingredients

- 2 and ½ pounds country style pork ribs, trimmed of fat
- ¼ cup fresh lime juice
- 1 tablespoon chili powder
- 1 tablespoon ground cumin
- 2 teaspoon salt
- ½ cup fresh cilantro, chopped

Directions

1. Add pork in slow cooker
2. Pour lime juice over pork and sprinkle chili powder, salt and cumin
3. Cover and cook on LOW for 8 hours
4. Transfer pork to cutting board and shred meat with two forks
5. Return pork to Slow Cooker and stir
6. Add chopped cilantro and serve
7. Enjoy!

Nutrition Values (per serving)

- Calories: 360
- Fat: 22g
- Carbohydrates: 2g
- **Protein: 37g**

Easy Beef Brisket

(Prepping time: 15 minutes\ Cooking time: 10 hours |For 8 servings)

Ingredients

- 1 (5 pound) beef brisket, trimmed
- 2 teaspoons garlic powder
- 2 teaspoons chili powder
- 2 teaspoons salt
- ½ teaspoon freshly ground black pepper
- ½ cup ketchup
- 1/3 cup apple cider vinegar
- 2 tablespoons Worcestershire sauce (Go for Gluten free brand such as French's Worcestershire Sauce)
- 2 teaspoons Dijon mustard
- 2 tablespoon stevia
- 1 teaspoon garlic powder

Directions

1. Place brisket in your Slow Cooker
2. Take a small bowl and add garlic powder, salt, chili powder, pepper and rub the brisket with seasoning
3. Take a medium bowl and whisk ketchup, apple cider vinegar, Worcestershire sauce, Dijon mustard, stevia and garlic powder
4. Pour sauce over brisket
5. Cover and cook on LOW for 10 hours
6. Transfer brisket to cutting board
7. Cut in thin slices across grain
8. Return brisket to Slow Cooker and stir with the sauce
9. Enjoy!

Nutrition Values (per serving)
- Calories: 818
- Fat: 63g
- Carbohydrates: 10g
- **Protein: 53g**

Dijon Pork Chops

(Prepping time: 10 minutes\ Cooking time: 8 hours |For 4 servings)

Ingredients

- 1 tablespoon extra-virgin olive oil
- 1 cup chicken broth
- 1 sweet onion, chopped
- ¼ cup Dijon mustard
- 1 teaspoon garlic, minced
- 1 teaspoon maple extract
- 4 boneless pork chops (4 ounce each)
- 1 cup cashew cream
- 1 teaspoon fresh thyme , chopped

Directions

1. Grease the insert of Slow Cooker with olive oil
2. Add broth, onion, garlic, Dijon mustard, maple extract to the Insert
3. Stir well
4. Add pork chops
5. Cover and cook on LOW for 8 hours
6. Stir in cashew cream
7. Serve with topping of thyme
8. Serve and enjoy!

Nutrition Values (per serving)

- Calories: 490
- Fat: 42g
- Carbohydrates: 5g
- **Protein: 22g**

Chapter 6: Healthy Vegan And Vegetarian Recipes

Hearty Asparagus Salad

(Prepping time: 10 minutes\ Cooking time: 20 minutes |For 4 servings)

Ingredients
- 1 lemon juice
- 2 salmon fillets
- 1 tablespoon champagne vinegar
- 1 tablespoon walnut oil
- 1 tablespoon Dijon mustard
- ¼ cup goat parmesan cheese, shredded
- ¼ cup fresh mint
- ¼ cup pine nuts, roasted
- ¼ teaspoon pepper
- 2 cups asparagus, shaved

Directions
1. Season salmon with salt and keep it on the side
2. Place a trivet in your Instant Pot
3. Place salmon over the trivet and close lid, cook on HIGH pressure for 15 minutes
4. Quick release pressure
5. Transfer salmon to platter and keep it on the side
6. Add asparagus around the salmon
7. Take a small bowl and mix lemon juice. Walnut oil, champagne vinegar, mustard and whisk well
8. Drizzle the dressing over salmon and asparagus

9. Garnish with pine nuts, pepper, mint and cheddar cheese
10. Serve and enjoy!

Nutrition Values (Per Serving)
- Calories: 323
- Fat: 21g
- Carbohydrates: 5g
- **Protein: 28g**

Multi-Colored Brussels

(Prepping time: 10 minutes\ Cooking time: 3 minutes |For 2 servings)

Ingredients

- 1 pound Brussels sprouts
- ¼ cup pine nuts, toasted
- 1 tablespoon extra-virgin olive oil
- ½ teaspoon salt
- 1 pepper, grated

Directions

1. Remove outer leaves of the Brussels and trim stems
2. Wash Brussels thoroughly
3. Cut the largest in half and cut the others in uniform sizes
4. Add a cup of water to your Instant Pot
5. Place steamer Basket
6. Add sprouts to your basket
7. Lock lid and cook on HIGH pressure for 3 minutes
8. Release pressure naturally over 10 minutes
9. Transfer sprouts to serving dish and toss with olive oil, salt and pepper
10. Sprinkle toasted pine nuts and enjoy!

Nutrition Values (Per Serving)

- Calories: 197
- Fat: 7g
- Carbohydrates: 22g
- Protein: 6g

Zucchini And Artichoke Platter

(Prepping time: 2 minutes\ Cooking time: 10 minutes |For 6 servings)

Ingredients

- 2 tablespoon coconut oil
- 1 bulb garlic, minced
- 1 large artichoke heart, cleaned sliced
- 2 medium zucchinis, sliced
- ½ cup vegetable broth
- Salt and pepper as needed

Directions

1. Set your pot to Saute mode and add oil, allow the oil the heat up
2. Add garlic and Saute until nicely fragrant
3. Add rest of the ingredients and stir
4. Lock lid and cook on HIGH pressure for 10 minutes
5. Quick release, serve an enjoy!

Nutrition Values (Per Serving)

- Calories: 33
- Fat: 3g
- Carbohydrates: 2g
- Protein: 0.57g

Heart "Beets" In A Pot

(Prepping time: 5 minutes\ Cooking time: 15 minutes |For 6 servings)

Ingredients
- 6 medium beets
- 1 cup water
- Salt and pepper as needed
- Balsamic vinegar
- Extra virgin olive oil

Directions
1. Wash the beets thoroughly and trim them to ½ inch long portions
2. Add a cup of water to your Instant Pot
3. Place steamer insert on top
4. Arrange beets in the Steamer Insert
5. Lock lid and cook on HIGH pressure for 15 minutes
6. Naturally release pressure over 10 minutes
7. Let the beets cool
8. Slice tops and slide skin off
9. Slice beets to uniform portions and season with salt and pepper
10. Add a splash of balsamic and let them sit for 30 minutes
11. Serve with a drizzle of olive oil
12. Enjoy!

Nutrition Values (Per Serving)
- Calories: 24
- Fat: 0g
- Carbohydrates: 5g
- **Protein: 1g**

A Platter Of Leafy Greens

(Prepping time: 5 minutes\ Cooking time: 20 minutes |For 4 servings)

Ingredients
- 1 bunch of assorted leafy greens

For Sauce
- ½ cup cashews, soaked for 10 minutes
- ¼ cup water
- 1 tablespoon lemon juice
- 1 teaspoon coconut aminos
- 1 clove, peeled
- 1/8 teaspoon salt

Directions
1. Drain the cashews and add to blender
2. Add water, lemon juice, garlic, salt and coconut aminos
3. Pulse until smooth
4. Transfer to bowl
5. Add ½ cup water to your Instant Pot
6. Place steamer basket to the pot and add greens
7. Lock lid and STEAM for 1 minute
8. Quick release pressure
9. Transfer steamer greens to strainer and extract excess water
10. Place greens into mixing bowl and add lemon garlic sauce
11. Toss and enjoy!

Nutrition Values (Per Serving)
- Calories: 77
- Fat: 5g
- Carbohydrates: 0g

- Protein: 2g

Simple Zucchini Pasta Pesto

(Prepping time: 3 minutes\ Cooking time: 10 minutes |For 4-6 servings)

Ingredients

- 1 tablespoon olive oil
- 1 onion, roughly chopped
- 2 and ½ pounds zucchini, chopped
- ½ cup water
- 1 and ½ teaspoon salt
- 1 bunch basil, picked off
- 2 garlic cloves, minced
- 1 tablespoon extra-virgin olive oil

Directions

1. Set your pot to Saute mode and add olive oil
2. Let the oil heat up, add onions and Saute for 4 minutes
3. Add salt, water and Zucchini
4. Lock lid and cook on HIGH pressure for 3 minutes
5. Release pressure naturally over 10 minutes
6. Add basil leaves, garlic
7. Puree using immersion blender
8. Pass Zucchini through a Spiralizer to form pasta
9. Mix with the sauce and enjoy!

Nutrition Values (Per Serving)

- Calories: 71
- Fat: 4.7g
- Carbohydrates: 7.5g
- **Protein: 1.2g**

Super Baked Apple Dish

(Prepping time: 10 minutes\ Cooking time: 4 hours 15 minutes |For 4 servings)

Ingredients

- 5 medium apples
- ½ teaspoon nutmeg powder
- ½ teaspoon cinnamon powder
- 2 drops stevia
- 1 cup walnuts
- Ghee for greasing

Directions

1. Peel the apples about fourth of the way down and remove cores and seeds
2. Take a bowl and add the remaining mixture and mix them well
3. Fill the peeled apples with the prepared mixture
4. Grease your Slow Cooker with ghee
5. Grease the outer part of your apples with ghee as well
6. Transfer apples to your Slow Cooker and put lid
7. Cook on LOW for 4 hours
8. Remove lid immediately and remove apples
9. Let them reach room temperature and serve
10. Enjoy!

Nutrition Values (per serving)

- Calories: 152
- Fat: 2g
- Carbohydrates: 35g
- **Protein: 1g**

Delicious Root Vegetable Dish

(Prepping time: 10 minutes\ Cooking time: 8 hours |For 4 servings)

Ingredients

- 4 Yukon Gold potatoes, chopped
- 2 russet potatoes, chopped
- 1 large parsnip, peeled and chopped
- 3 large carrots, peeled and chopped
- 2 onions, chopped
- 2 garlic cloves, minced
- 2 tablespoons olive oil
- ¼ cup roasted vegetable broth
- ½ teaspoon salt
- 1 teaspoon dried thyme leaves

Directions

1. Add the listed ingredients to your Slow Cooker
2. Stir well
3. Cover and cook on LOW for 7-8 hours
4. Stir hash and enjoy

Nutrition Values (per serving)

- Calories: 150
- Fat: 0g
- Carbohydrates: 28g
- **Protein: 3g**

Feisty Potato Grain

(Prepping time: 20 minutes\ Cooking time: 9 hour |For 8 servings)

Ingredients

- 6 Yukon Gold Potatoes, thinly sliced
- 3 sweet potatoes, thinly sliced and peeled
- 2 onions, thinly sliced
- 4 garlic cloves, minced
- 3 tablespoons almond flour
- 4 cups almond milk
- 1 and 1/2 cups roasted veggie broth
- 3 tablespoons ghee
- 1 teaspoon dried thyme leaves
- 1 and ½ cup cashew cream

Directions

1. Grease your slow cooker with olive oil
2. Layer potatoes, onion and garlic
3. Take a large bowl and add flour, ½ cup milk and stir well
4. Stir in broth, ghee, thyme leaves
5. Pour milk mix over potatoes
6. Top with cashew cream
7. Cover and cook for 7-9 hours
8. Enjoy!

Nutrition Values (per serving)

- Calories: 415
- Fat: 22g
- Carbohydrates: 42g
- **Protein: 17g**

Caramelized Onion With Dope Garlic

(Prepping time: 20 minutes\ Cooking time: 8-10 hour |For 3 servings)

Ingredients

- 10 large yellow onions, peeled and sliced
- 20 garlic cloves, peeled
- ¼ cup olive oil
- ¼ teaspoon salt
- 2 tablespoons balsamic vinegar
- 1 teaspoon dried thyme leaves

Directions

1. Add the listed ingredients to your Slow Cooker
2. Stir well
3. Cover and cook on LOW for 8-10 hours
4. Serve and enjoy!

Nutrition Values (per serving)

- Calories: 109
- Fat: 4g
- Carbohydrates: 16g
- **Protein: 2g**

Delicious Ginger Sweet Potatoes

(Prepping time: 10 minutes\ Cooking time: 3-4 hours |For 8 servings)

Ingredients

- 2 and ½ pound sweet potatoes, peeled
- 1 cup water
- 1 tablespoon fresh ginger, grated
- ½ teaspoon ginger, minced
- ½ tablespoon ghee

Directions

1. Peel the potatoes and quarter them
2. Add them to the slow cooker
3. Add water, fresh ginger and ginger
4. **Stir well**
5. Cook on HIGH for 3-4 hours until the potatoes are tender
6. Add ghee and mash them
7. Serve immediately and enjoy!

Nutrition Values (per serving)

- Calories: 100
- Fat: 0.5g
- Carbohydrates: 23g
- Protein: 2g

Chapter 7: Flavored Soup And Stews Recipes

Smoked Paprika Soup

(Prepping time: 10 minutes\ Cooking time: 25 minutes | For 6 servings)

Ingredients

- 1 medium onion, chopped finely
- 3 garlic cloves, minced
- 2 teaspoons cumin
- 1 and ½ teaspoon smoked paprika
- 2 carrots, sliced
- 2 celery stalks
- 1 bunch spinach
- 8 cups water
- 1 teaspoon salt
- 1 teaspoon pepper

Directions

1. Set your pot to Saute mode and add oil, garlic, onion, spices, carrots, celery and Saute for 5 minutes until the onions are translucent
2. Add enough water to cover them
3. Lock lid and cook on HIGH pressure for 10 minutes (on Soup Mode)
4. Release pressure naturally over 10 minutes
5. Open lid and set pot to Saute mode and cook for 5 minutes
6. Add smoked paprika, cumin and season with salt and pepper
7. Serve hot and enjoy!

Nutrition Values (Per Serving)

- Calories: 179
- Fat: 1.2g
- Carbohydrates: 31g
- **Protein: 12g**

Lovely Cabbage And Leek Delight

(Prepping time: 10 minutes\ Cooking time: 25 minutes |For 4 servings)

Ingredients

- 2 tablespoon coconut oil
- ½ head cabbage, chopped
- 3-4 celery ribs, diced
- 2-3 leeks, cleaned and chopped
- 1 bell pepper, diced
- 2-3 carrots, diced
- 2-3 garlic cloves, minced
- 4 cups chicken broth
- 1 teaspoon Italian seasoning
- 1 teaspoon Creole seasoning
- Black pepper as needed
- 2-3 cups mixed salad greens

Directions

1. Set your pot to Saute mode and add coconut oil
2. Allow the oil to heat up
3. Add the veggies (except salad greens) starting from the carrot, making sure to stir it well after each vegetable addition
4. Make sure to add the garlic last
5. Season with Italian seasoning, black pepper and Creole seasoning
6. Add broth and lock up the lid
7. Cook on SOUP mode for 20 minutes
8. Release the pressure naturally and add salad greens, stir well and allow it to sit for a while
9. Allow for a few minutes to wilt the veggies
10. Season with a bit of flavored vinegar and pepper and enjoy!

Nutrition Values (Per Serving)
- Calories: 32
- Fat: 0g
- Carbohydrates: 4g
- **Protein: 2g**

Tongue Teasing Mushroom Soup

(Prepping time: 10 minutes\ Cooking time: 10 minutes |For 4 servings)

Ingredients

- 1 pound mushroom, sliced
- 2 ounce shiitake mushrooms, chopped
- 1 shallot, chopped
- 4 garlic cloves, chopped
- 2 tablespoon almond butter
- 2 cups water
- ½ cup cashew cream
- Salt and pepper to taste

Directions

1. Add the listed ingredients to your Instant Pot
2. Season with salt and pepper and stir
3. Lock lid and cook on HIGH pressure for 10 minutes
4. Release pressure naturally over 10 minutes
5. Use an immersion blender to puree the mixture
6. Serve and enjoy!

Nutrition Values (Per Serving)

- Calories: 70
- Fat: 6g
- Carbohydrates: 4g
- Protein: 2g

Light Carrot Soup

(Prepping time: 10 minutes\ Cooking time: 15 minutes |For 4 servings)

Ingredients

- 1 tablespoon ghee
- ½ yellow onion, chopped
- 3 cloves garlic, minced
- 1 tablespoon curry powder
- 1 teaspoon cayenne pepper
- 1 and ½ cups vegetable broth
- 8-10 large carrots, peeled and chopped
- 1 can of 14 ounces unsweetened coconut milk

Directions

1. Set your pot to Saute mode and add ghee
2. Add onion and garlic and Saute for 3-5 minutes
3. Add reset of the ingredients except coconut milk and stir
4. Lock lid and cook on HIGH pressure for 15 minutes
5. Release pressure naturally over 10 minutes
6. Use and immersion blender to smoothen the soup
7. Serve hot and enjoy!

Nutrition Values (Per Serving)

- Calories: 179
- Fat: 1.2g
- Carbohydrates: 31g
- **Protein: 12g**

Inspiring Broccoli And Leek Soup

(Prepping time: 5 minutes\ Cooking time: 5 minutes |For 4 servings)

Ingredients

- 2 tablespoons ghee
- 3 medium leeks, white parts only
- 2 shallots, chopped
- 1 large head broccoli, cut into florets
- 4 cups vegetable broth
- 1 cup unsweetened coconut milk
- Salt and pepper to taste
- ¼ cup walnuts, toasted
- ¼ cup coconut cream

Directions

1. Set your pot to Saute mode and add ghee
2. Add shallots, leeks and cook for 4-6 minutes until tender
3. Add broccoli and Saute for 5-6 minutes
4. Add vegetable broth and stir
5. Lock lid and cook on HIGH pressure for 5 minutes
6. Release pressure naturally over 10 minutes
7. Puree using immersion blender
8. Stir in coconut milk and season with more salt and pepper if needed
9. Ladle into bowls and top with walnuts and a drizzle of coconut cream
10. Enjoy!

Nutrition Values (Per Serving)

- Calories: 179
- Fat: 1.2g
- Carbohydrates: 31g
- **Protein: 12g**

Elegant Cauliflower Soup

(Prepping time: 5 minutes\ Cooking time: 25 minutes |For 6 servings)

Ingredients

- 2 tablespoons extra virgin olive oil
- 1 onion, chopped
- 2 teaspoons ginger, finely chopped
- 2 garlic cloves, chopped
- 2 bunch cauliflower, florets
- 2 teaspoon curry powder
- 1 teaspoon cumin
- ½ teaspoon salt
- 2 cups coconut milk
- 6 cups vegetable stock
- Coriander leaves
- 4 almonds, blanched and sliced

Directions

1. Set your pot to Saute mode and add olive oil, allow the oil to heat up
2. Add onion and cook for 2-3 minutes
3. Add garlic cloves, ginger, cauliflower florets and Saute for 4 minutes
4. Add spices such as cumin and salt
5. Add almond milk and vegetable stock
6. Lock lid and cook on SOUP mode for 10 minutes
7. Quick release the pressure
8. Open lid and puree the soup using an immersion blender until you have a smooth soup
9. Transfer soup to serving bowls and top with coriander leaves and almond
10. Enjoy!

Nutrition Values (Per Serving)
- Calories: 260
- Fat: 24g
- Carbohydrates: 10g
- **Protein: 4g**

Awesome Beef Stew

(Prepping time: 10 minutes\ Cooking time: 40 minutes |For 6 servings)

Ingredients

- 2 pounds beef roast, fat removed and cubed
- 4 carrots, cubed
- 2 celery stalks, chopped
- 1 yellow onion, chopped
- 2 tablespoons tapioca flour
- ½ cup tomato juice

Directions

1. Add beef, carrots, celery, flour, onion and tomato juice to the pot and toss well
2. Close lid and cook on LOW pressure for 35 minutes
3. Release pressure naturally over 10 minutes
4. Open lid and divide into bowls
5. Serve and enjoy!

Nutrition Values (Per Serving)

- Calories : 261
- Fat :6g
- Carbohydrates : 18g
- Protein : 8g

Blissful Turkey Spinach Soup

(Prepping time: 10 minutes\ Cooking time: 8 hours |For 4 servings)

Ingredients

- 4 cups baby spinach
- 1 tablespoon oregano
- 1 tablespoon ginger, minced
- 1 cup turkey meat, boiled and cubed
- Salt
- Red chili flakes

Directions

1. Add all the listed ingredients to your Slow Cooker except meat
2. Add enough water to cover them
3. Close lid and cook on LOW for 7 hours
4. Let the soup sit for a while
5. Open lid and use immersion blender to smoothen the soup
6. Add cooked turkey cubes and close lid
7. Cook on LOW for 1 hour more
8. Stir and serve
9. Enjoy!

Nutrition Values (per serving)

- Calories: 215
- Fat: 7g
- Carbohydrates: 19g
- **Protein: 18g**

Bacon And Spinach Soup

(Prepping time: 10 minutes\ Cooking time: 3 hours 15 minutes |For 4 servings)

Ingredients

- 3 cups baby spinach
- ½ cup sweet potato
- ½ cup broccoli florets
- 2 tablespoons ginger, minced
- 2 tablespoons garlic cloves, minced
- Salt as needed
- Red chili flakes as needed
- 3 bacon slices
- 3 cups vegetable broth

Directions

1. Cook bacon slices in your Slow Cooker until they are crispy, keep them on the side
2. Add the remaining ingredients in the leftover bacon grease in your Slow Cooker
3. Close lid and cook on LOW for 3 hours
4. Let the soup sit for a while
5. Crumbled the crisped bacon slices and add them to the soup
6. Stir well and cook for 5 minutes more (lid off)
7. Season accordingly and enjoy!

Nutrition Values (per serving)

- Calories: 339
- Fat: 18g
- Carbohydrates: 32g
- **Protein: 13g**

Amazing Sausage Soup

(Prepping time: 10 minutes\ Cooking time: 6 hours 5 minutes |For 4 servings)

Ingredients

- 1 cup onion, chopped
- 1 cup Sautéed sausages, cubed
- 2 tablespoon ginger, minced
- Salt as needed
- Red chili flakes as needed
- 3 cups mushroom stock

Directions

1. Add the listed ingredients to your Slow Cooker
2. Close lid and cook on LOW for 6 hours
3. Let the soup sit for a while
4. Open lid and stir thoroughly
5. Let it cook for 5 minutes more without lid
6. Serve with your desired seasoning
7. Enjoy!

Nutrition Values (per serving)

- Calories: 269
- Fat: 9g
- Carbohydrates: 39g
- **Protein: 10g**

Authentic Chard Soup

(Prepping time: 10 minutes\ Cooking time: 3 hours 5 minutes |For 4 servings)

Ingredients

- 2 and ½ cups Swiss chard, chopped
- 2 tablespoons ginger, minced
- 1 cup onion, chopped
- 1 teaspoon oregano
- Salt as needed
- Red chili flakes as needed

Directions

1. Add the listed ingredients to your Slow Cooker
2. Add enough water to cover the ingredients
3. Close lid and cook on MEDIUM for 3 hours
4. Let it sit for a while
5. Open lid and use immersion blender to blend the soup into a creamy texture
6. Stir and enjoy with more seasoning if needed

Nutrition Values (per serving)

- Calories: 284
- Fat: 19g
- Carbohydrates: 13g
- **Protein: 15g**

Ultimate Cauliflower Soup

(Prepping time: 10 minutes\ Cooking time: 3 hours 5 minutes |For 4 servings)

Ingredients

- 1 tablespoon ginger, minced
- 1 teaspoon lemon juice
- 3 cups cauliflower florets
- ½ teaspoon hot sauce
- Salt as needed
- Red chili flakes as needed

Directions

1. Add the listed ingredients to your Slow Cooker
2. Add 2 cups of water
3. Stir and put lid
4. Cook on MEDIUM for 3 hours
5. Let it sit for a while
6. Remove lid and blend using an immersion blender to make the soup creamy and smooth
7. Stir the soup well and seasoning according to your taste
8. Serve and enjoy!

Nutrition Values (per serving)

- Calories: 412
- Fat: 18g
- Carbohydrates: 43g
- **Protein: 22g**

Chapter 8: Great Snack And Desserts Recipes

Whole Roasted Garlic

(Prepping time: 5 minutes\ Cooking time: 20 minutes |For 6 servings)

Ingredients
- 3 large garlic bulbs
- 1 cup water

Directions
11. Slice off ¼ of the garlic bulb from top, keeping the bulb intact
12. Add water to your Instant Pot and a steamer trivet
13. Transfer garlic bulb on rack and lock lid, cook on HIGH pressure for 5-6 minutes
14. Naturally release the pressure over 10 minutes
15. Transfer the soft garlic to grill rack in your oven and roast for 5 minutes
16. Serve and enjoy!

Nutrition Values (Per Serving)
- Calories: 8
- Fat: 0g
- Carbohydrates: 1.5g
- **Protein: 0g**

Juicy Caramelized Onion

(Prepping time: 5 minutes\ Cooking time: 15 minutes |For 4 servings)

Ingredients

- 3 large onion bulbs
- 1 cup water

Directions

1. Slice ¼ of onion bulb from top, keeping the bulb intact
2. Add water to your Instant Pot and a steamer trivet
3. Transfer onion bulb on rack and lock lid, cook on HIGH pressure for 5-6 minutes
4. Naturally release the pressure over 10 minutes
5. Transfer the soft onion to grill rack in your oven and roast for 5 minutes
6. Serve and enjoy!

Nutrition Values (Per Serving)

- Calories: 6
- Fat: 0g
- Carbohydrates: 1.4g
- **Protein: 0.2g**

Hearty Steamed Sweet Potatoes

(Prepping time: 10 minutes\ Cooking time: 10 minutes |For 6 servings)

Ingredients
- 10 baby sweet potatoes
- 1 and ½ cups water
- Salt and pepper as needed

Directions
1. Add 1 and ½ cups water to your Instant Pot
2. Place metal trivet inside
3. Wash the sweet potatoes and transfer to metal trivet
4. Lock lid and cook on HIGH pressure for 10 minutes
5. Naturally release the pressure over 10 minutes
6. Season potatoes with salt and pepper, grill in oven for 5 minutes for crispy potatoes

Nutrition Values (Per Serving)
- Calories: 83
- Fat: 0g
- Carbohydrates: 18g
- **Protein: 1.7g**

Maple Dressed Carrots

(Prepping time: 5 minutes\ Cooking time: 4 minutes |For 4 servings)

Ingredients

- 2 pound of carrots
- ¼ cup of raisins
- Pepper as needed
- 1 cup of water
- 1 tablespoon of coconut butter
- 1 tablespoon of maple syrup

Directions

1. Wash and peel the carrots, sliced them
2. Add carrots, water and raisins to your Instant Pot
3. Lock lid and cook on HIGH pressure for 4 minutes
4. Release the pressure naturally over 10 minutes
5. Strain the carrots and add coconut butter and maple syrup
6. Mix in the strained carrots and toss them
7. Add raisins and toss again
8. Season with a bit of pepper
9. Serve and enjoy!

Nutrition Values (Per Serving)

- Calories: 228
- Fat: 8g
- Carbohydrates: 36g
- Protein: 4g

Lovely Potato Hash

(Prepping time: 10 minutes\ Cooking time: 4 hours |For 2 servings)

Ingredients
- 1 medium orange pepper, sliced and diced, deseeded
- 1 medium yellow pepper, sliced and diced, deseeded
- 10 and ½ ounces sweet potato
- 1 tablespoon coconut oil
- 1 teaspoon garlic puree
- 1 teaspoon thyme
- 1 teaspoon mustard powder
- Salt and pepper as needed

Directions
1. Dice the vegetables and potatoes and transfer to your Slow Cooker
2. Add coconut oil and seasoning
3. Mix
4. **Cover with lid and cook on LOW for 4 hours**
5. Serve and enjoy!

Nutrition Values (per serving)
- Calories: 270
- Fat: 10g
- Carbohydrates: 39g
- **Protein: 5g**

Herbed Mushrooms

(Prepping time: 20 minutes\ Cooking time: 4 hours |For 4 servings)

Ingredients
- 24 ounce cremini mushrooms
- 4 garlic cloves, minced
- ½ teaspoon dried basil
- ½ teaspoon dried oregano
- 2 tablespoon parsley, minced
- 1 bay leaf
- 1 cup vegetable stock
- ¼ cup coconut milk
- 2 tablespoon ghee
- Sea salt as needed
- Freshly ground black pepper

Directions
1. Add the mushrooms, herbs and garlic to your slow cooker
2. Pour vegetable stock to the cooker and season
3. Cover and cook on LOW for 4 hours
4. **Add coconut milk, stir and cook for a while until it is warm**
5. Discard the bay leaf and season again
6. Serve!

Nutrition Values (per serving)
- Calories: 190
- Fat: 1g
- Carbohydrates: 40g
- **Protein: 8g**

Conclusion

I cannot express how honored I am that you found my book interesting and informative to read to the end.

Thank you once more for purchasing this book and I hope you had as much fun reading it as I had writing it.

I bid you farewell and encourage you to move forward with your amazing Lectin Free Diet journey!

www.ingramcontent.com/pod-product-compliance
Lightning Source LLC
Chambersburg PA
CBHW071440070526
44578CB00001B/164